William H Walter

A Manual of Church Music

Containing a choice selection of chants and metrical tunes, designed for use in

public and private worship

William H Walter

A Manual of Church Music
Containing a choice selection of chants and metrical tunes, designed for use in public and private worship

ISBN/EAN: 9783337290276

Printed in Europe, USA, Canada, Australia, Japan

Cover: Foto ©Thomas Meinert / pixelio.de

More available books at **www.hansebooks.com**

A MANUAL

OF

CHURCH MUSIC:

CONTAINING A CHOICE SELECTION OF

CHANTS AND METRICAL TUNES,

DESIGNED FOR USE IN

PUBLIC AND PRIVATE WORSHIP,

COMPILED BY

WILLIAM H. WALTER,

Organist and Director of the Choir of Trinity Chapel, and Organist of Columbia College, New York.

"Sing ye praises with understanding."

[SECOND EDITION.]

New York:
PUBLISHED BY S. T. GORDON, 538 BROADWAY.

AND ALSO BY THE

GENERAL PROTESTANT EPISCOPAL SUNDAY SCHOOL UNION, AND CHURCH BOOK SOCIETY, 762 BROADWAY.

1863.

Entered according to Act of Congress in the year 1863, by
THEO. H. SMITH,
in the Clerk's office of the United States District Court for the Southern District of New York.

PREFACE.

This compilation of Chants and Metrical Tunes, is now put forth in response to numerous and oft repeated wishes of friends, both far and near, and, though perhaps rather hastily prepared, will, it is hoped, prove acceptable, being the result of much labor and experience in the cause of Church Music.

The Chants, which are few in number, are, most of them, already well known to the public, while those which are comparatively new, have been well tested by actual use in the Church.

The selection of Metrical Tunes comprises a wider range and variety. In this part the compiler has endeavored to avoid the extremes of too strict adherence to the Choral style, or, too great a leaning towards the more popular melodies of the secular school. Many tunes are here admitted which the compiler does not heartily approve, and some others which will not be generally acceptable until our Choirs are differently constituted from those now in vogue, and a purer taste in such matters shall prevail.

The words which are set to the Tunes are intended, with a few exceptions, rather for convenience in Choir-practice than as examples of proper adaptation. But, those instances where a whole Psalm or Hymn is printed, may be taken as indications of special fitness between words and music. The Tunes are numbered, in order that they may be announced by the Minister when he gives out the Psalm or Hymn to be sung. This, it is hoped, will be of great advantage, and prevent confusion in Churches where congregational singing prevails.

The Chants and Tunes composed by Dr. HODGES, are taken by his permission from the "National Lyre," and are regarded as strictly copy-right, the right to publish having been purchased at a considerable outlay.

To his friend, Mr. THEO. H. SMITH, whose excellent taste is only equalled by his noble liberality, the compiler desires here to acknowledge his obligations for assistance in the publication of this work.

WILLIAM H. WALTER.

New York, January, 1863.

Morning Prayer.

4. DOUBLE CHANT.

VENITE, EXULTEMUS DOMINO.

1. O come, let us sing .... un-	to the	LORD :
2. Let us come before his presence	with thanks-	giving :
3. For the LORD is... a	great	God :
4. In his hand are all the corners	of the	earth :
5. The sea is his	and he	made it :
6. O come, let us worship..	and fall	down :
7. For he is .... the	Lord our	God :
8. O worship the LORD in....................................the	beauty of	holiness :
*9. For he cometh, for he cometh .... to	judge the	earth :
10. Glory be to the Father	and to the	Son :
11. As it was in the beginning, is now, ...and	ev - er	shall be :

5. DOUBLE CHANT.

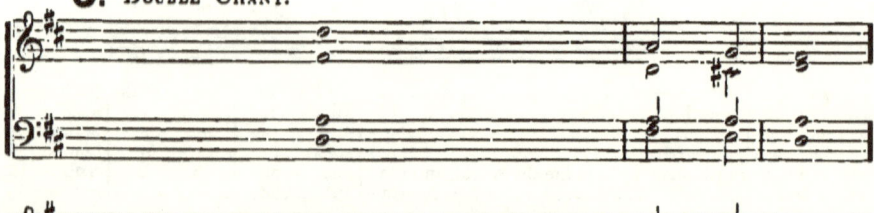

* The 9th verse, " *For he cometh,*" &c., should be sung to the last h..." of the chant.

Morning Prayer.

Dr. Hayes.

let us heartily rejoice	in the	strength of	our	sal-	vation.	2.
and show ourselves		glad	in	him with	psalms.	3.
and a great		King	a-	bove all	gods.	4.
and the strength of	the	hills	is	his	also.	5.
and his hands	pre-	pared	the	dry	land.	6.
and kneel	be-	fore	the	Lord our	Maker.	7.
and we are the people of his pasture and	the	sheep	of	his	hand.	8.
let the whole earth		stand	in	awe	of him.	9.
and with righteousness to judge the world, and the	peo - ple	with	his	truth.	10.
and		to	the	Ho - ly	Ghost.	11.
world	with-	out	end,	A - - -	MEN.

Dr. Boyce.

Morning Prayer.

6. DOUBLE CHANT.

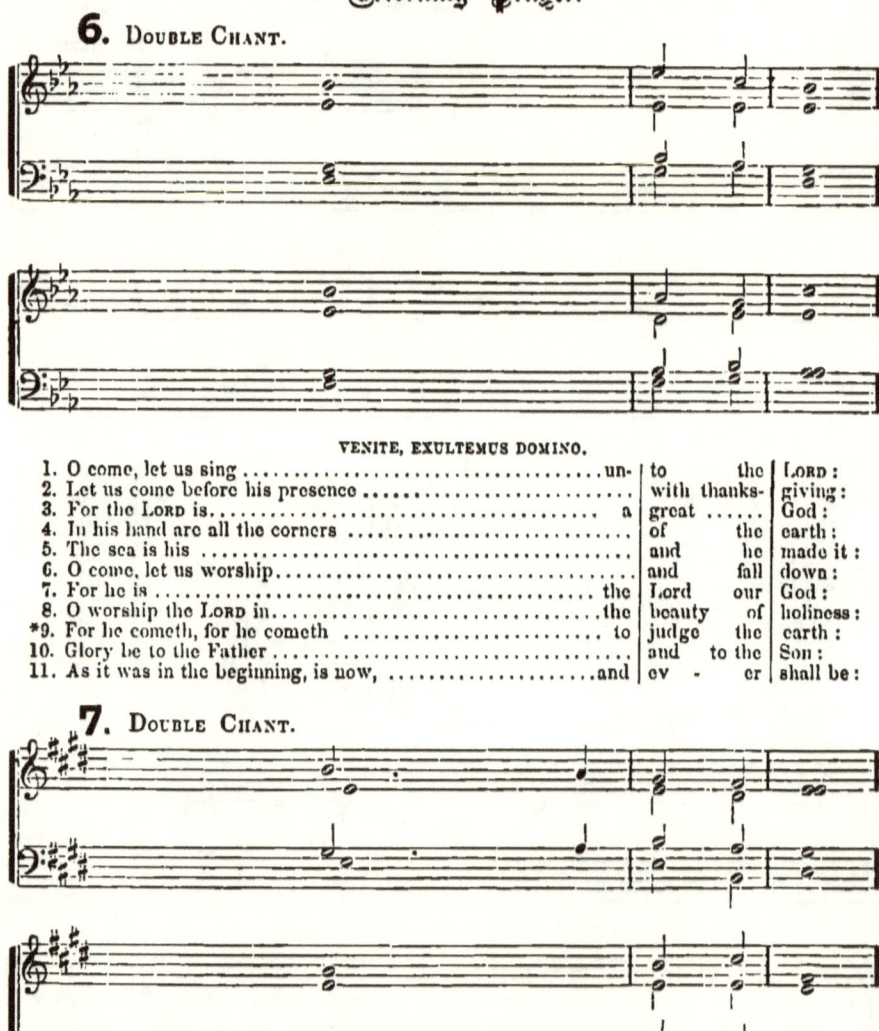

VENITE, EXULTEMUS DOMINO.

1. O come, let us sing .... un- | to the | LORD :
2. Let us come before his presence .... | with thanks- | giving :
3. For the LORD is .... a | great ...... | God :
4. In his hand are all the corners .... | of the | earth :
5. The sea is his .... | and he | made it :
6. O come, let us worship .... | and fall | down :
7. For he is .... the | Lord our | God :
8. O worship the LORD in ....the | beauty of | holiness :
*9. For he cometh, for he cometh .... to | judge the | earth :
10. Glory be to the Father .... | and to the | Son :
11. As it was in the beginning, is now, ...and | ev - er | shall be :

7. DOUBLE CHANT.

* The 9th verse, "For he cometh," &c., should be sung to the last half of the chant.

10   Gloria in Excelsis.

8. TRIPLE CHANT.

1. Glory be...to | God on | high;
2. We praise thee, we bless thee,.....................we | wor - ship | thee,

3. O Lord God,... | heaven - ly | King,
4. O Lord, the only-begotten Son,................... | Je - sus | Christ;

5. That takest away.....................................the | sins of the | world,
6. Thou that takest away.............................the | sins of the | world,
7. Thou that takest away.............................the | sins of the | world,
8. Thou that sittest at the right hand.............of | God the | Father,

9. For thou only.. | art .... | holy;
10. Thou only, O Christ, with.........................the | Ho - ly | Ghost;

Gloria in Excelsis.

Morning Prayer.

9. DOUBLE CHANT.

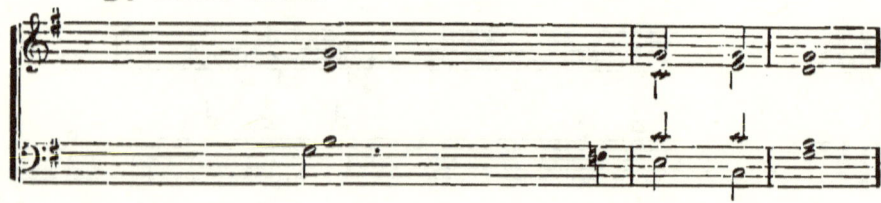

TE DEUM LAUDAMUS.

1. We praise	thee, O	God;
3. To thee all Angels	cry a -	loud;
5. Holy, ...	Ho - - ly,	Holy,
7. The glorious company of the Apostles	praise	thee,
9. The Father of ....an	Infi - nite	Majesty;
11. Thou	art the	King
13. When thou tookest upon thee to .... de-	liv - er	man,
15. Thou sittest at the right	hand of	God,
17. We therefore pray thee	help thy	servants,
19. O Lord, ...	save thy	people,
21. Day .... by		day
23. Vouch - - - - - - - -	safe, O	Lord,
25. O Lord, let thy mercy	be up-	on us,

2. All the earth .... doth	wor - ship	thee,
4. To thee Cherubim .... and	Ser - a -	phim
6. Heaven .... and	earth are	full,
8. The noble army of Martyrs	praise	thee.
10. Also .... the	Ho - - ly	Ghost,
12. Thou art the ev - - - - - - - er-	last - ing	Son
14. When thou hadst overcome .... the	sharpness of	death,
16. We believe .... that	thou shalt	come
18. Make them to be numbered	with thy	Saints,
20. Gov - - - - - - - -	- ern	them,
22. And .... we	worship thy	Name,
24. O Lord, ... have	mercy up	on us,
26. O Lord, in thee	have I	trusted,

Morning Prayer.

Dr. HODGES.

(After the First Lesson.)

we acknowledge	thee	to	be the	Lord. 2.
the Heavens, ...and	all	the	Powers there-	in. 4.
Lord	God	of	Sa - ba-	oth. 6.
The goodly fellowship of ....the	Pro - phets	praise		thee. 8.
Thine adorable, ...	true,	and	on - ly	Son; 10.
of	Glo - ry,	O		Christ. 12.
thou didst humble thyself to ....be	born	of	a	Virgin. 14.
in ....the	Glo - ry	of	the	Father. 16.
whom thou hast redeem - - - - ed	with	thy	pre - cious	blood. 18.
and	bless	....	thine	heritage.20.
we	mag - ni-	fy		thee. 22.
to keep ....us	this	day	with - out	sin. 24.
as ....our	trust	is	- in	thee. 26.

the	Fa - ther	ev - er -	lasting.	3.
con - - - - - - - - - -	tin - ual-	ly do	cry,	5.
of ....the	Majes - ty	of thy	Glory.	7.
The Holy Church throughout all the world,......	doth ac	know - ledge	thee;	9.
the	Com -	- fort-	er.	11.
of	...... the	Fa -	- ther.	13.
thou didst open the Kingdom ....of	Heaven to	all be-	lievers.	15.
to	be	our	Judge.	17.
in	glo ry	ev - er	lasting.	19.
and	lift them	up for	ever.	21.
ever	world	with - out	end.	23
have	mer - cy	up - on	us.	25
let me	nev - er	be con-	founded.	

Morning Prayer.

10. Double Chant.

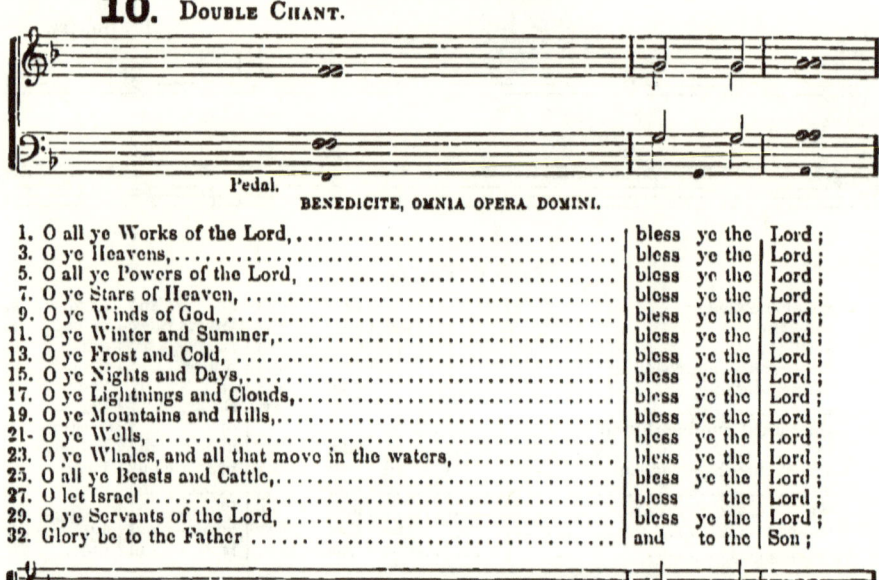

Pedal.

BENEDICITE, OMNIA OPERA DOMINI.

1. O all ye Works of the Lord,	bless	ye the	Lord;
3. O ye Heavens,	bless	ye the	Lord;
5. O all ye Powers of the Lord,	bless	ye the	Lord;
7. O ye Stars of Heaven,	bless	ye the	Lord;
9. O ye Winds of God,	bless	ye the	Lord;
11. O ye Winter and Summer,	bless	ye the	Lord;
13. O ye Frost and Cold,	bless	ye the	Lord;
15. O ye Nights and Days,	bless	ye the	Lord;
17. O ye Lightnings and Clouds,	bless	ye the	Lord;
19. O ye Mountains and Hills,	bless	ye the	Lord;
21. O ye Wells,	bless	ye the	Lord;
23. O ye Whales, and all that move in the waters,	bless	ye the	Lord;
25. O all ye Beasts and Cattle,	bless	ye the	Lord;
27. O let Israel	bless	the	Lord;
29. O ye Servants of the Lord,	bless	ye the	Lord;
32. Glory be to the Father	and	to the	Son;

2. O ye Angels of the Lord,	bless	ye the	Lord;
4. O ye Waters that be above the firmament,	bless	ye the	Lord;
6. O ye Sun and Moon,	bless	ye the	Lord;
8. O ye Showers and Dew,	bless	ye the	Lord;
10. O ye Fire and Heat,	bless	ye the	Lord;
12. O ye Dews and Frosts,	bless	ye the	Lord;
14. O ye Ice and Snow,	bless	ye the	Lord;
16. O ye Light and Darkness,	bless	ye the	Lord;
18. O let the Earth	bless	the	Lord;
20. O all ye Green Things upon the earth,	bless	ye the	Lord;
22. O ye Seas and Floods,	bless	ye the	Lord;
24. O all ye Fowls of the Air,	bless	ye the	Lord;
26. O ye Children of Men,	bless	ye the	Lord;
28. O ye Priests of the Lord,	bless	ye the	Lord;
30. O ye Spirits and Souls of the Righteous,	bless	ye the	Lord;
31. O ye holy and humble Men of heart,	bless	ye the	Lord;
33. As it was in the beginning, is now, and	ev	- er	shall be;

Morning Prayer.

15

Dr. Bennett.

(After the First Lesson, instead of the Te Deum.)

praise him, ...and	magni -	fy	him	for ever. 2.
praise him, ...and	magni -	fy	him	for ever. 4.
praise him, ...and	magni -	fy	him	for ever. 6.
praise him, ...and	magni -	fy	him	for ever. 8.
praise him, ...and	magni -	fy	him	for ever. 10.
praise him, ...and	magni -	fy	him	for ever. 12.
praise him, ...and	magni -	fy	him	for ever. 14.
praise him, ...and	magni -	fy	him	for ever. 16.
praise him, ...and	magni -	fy	him	for ever. 18.
praise him, ...and	magni -	fy	him	for ever. 20.
praise him, ...and	magni -	fy	him	for ever. 22.
praise him, ...and	magni -	fy	him	for ever. 24.
praise him, ...and	magni -	fy	him	for ever. 26.
praise him, ...and	magni -	fy	him	for ever. 28.
praise him, ...and	magni -	fy	him	for ever. 30.
and	to	the	Ho -	ly Ghost; 33.

praise him, ...and	magni -	fy	him	for ever. 3.
praise him, ...and	magni -	fy	him	for ever. 5.
praise him, ...and	magni -	fy	him	for ever. 7.
praise him, ...and	magni -	fy	him	for ever. 9.
praise him, ...and	magni -	fy	him	for ever. 11.
praise him, ...and	magni -	fy	him	for ever. 13.
praise him, ...and	magni -	fy	him	for ever. 15.
praise him, ...and	magni -	fy	him	for ever. 17.
yea, let it praise him, ...and	magni -	fy	him	for ever. 19.
praise him, ...and	magni -	fy	him	for ever. 21.
praise him, ...and	magni -	fy	him	for ever. 23.
praise him, ...and	magni -	fy	him	for ever. 25.
praise him, ...and	magni -	fy	him	for ever. 27.
praise him, ...and	magni -	fy	him	for ever. 29.
praise him, ...and	magni -	fy	him	for ever. 31.
praise him, ...and	magni -	fy	him	for ever. 32.
world ....with-	out	end.	A - - -	MEN.

Morning Prayer.

11. DOUBLE CHANT.

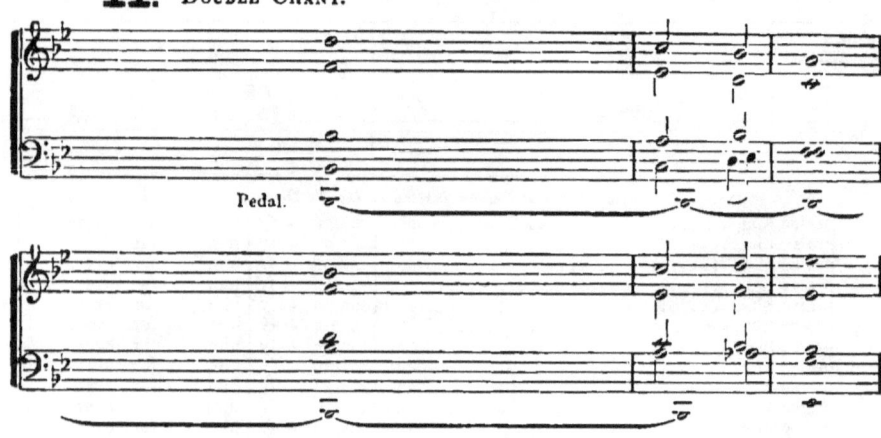

JUBILATE DEO. Psalm c.

1. O be joyful in the LORD...............................	all	ye	lands :
2. Be ye sure that the LORD	he	is	God :
3. O go your way into his gates with thanksgiving, and into his ..	courts	with	praise :
4. For the LORD is gracious, his mercy .... is	ev	- er	lasting :
5. Glory be to the Father	and	to the	Son :
6. As it was in the beginning, is now, ... and	ev	- er	shall be :

12. DOUBLE CHANT.

Morning Prayer.

Dr. Jackson.

(*After the Second Lesson.*)

serve the Lord with gladness, and come before his	pre - sence	with a	song.	2
it is he that hath made us, and not we ourselves, we are his people	and the	sheep of his	pasture.	3
be thankful unto him .... and	speak good	of his	Name.	4
and his truth endureth from gener - - -	ation to	gen - er -	ation.	5
and	to the	Ho - ly	Ghost.	6
world .... with	out end	A - - -	men.	

Dean Aldrich.

Morning Prayer.

13. Double Chant.

JUBILATE DEO. Psalm c.

1. O be joyful in the LORD....................................	all	ye	lands :
2. Be ye sure that the LORD	he	is	God :
3. O go your way into his gates with thanksgiving, and into his ..	courts	with	praise :
4. For the LORD is gracious, his mercy ....is	ev	- er	lasting :
5. Glory be to the Father	and	to the	Son :
6. As it was in the beginning, is now, ...and	ev	- er	shall be :

14. Double Chant.

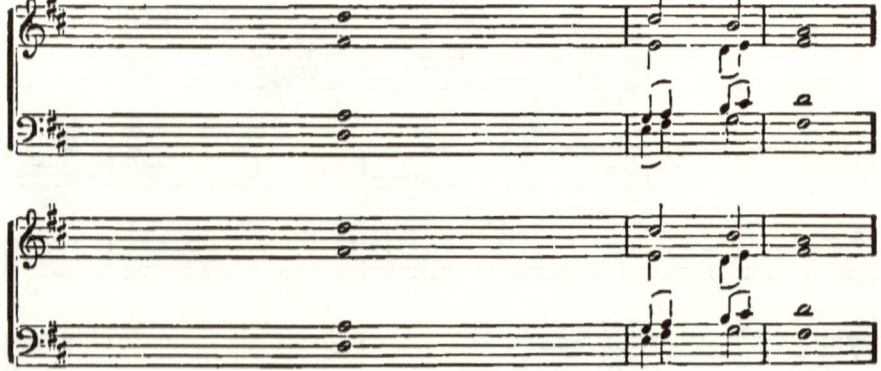

Morning Prayer.

J. Pratt.

(After the Second Lesson.)

· serve the Lord with gladness, and come before his	pre - sence	with a	song.	2.
it is he that hath made us, and not we ourselves, we are his people	and the	sheep of his	pasture.	3.
be thankful unto him .... and	speak good	of his	Name.	4.
and his truth endureth from gener - - - -	ation to	gen - er-	ation.	5.
and	to the	Ho - ly	Ghost.	6.
world ....with	out end.	A - - -	men.	

Battishill.

Morning Prayer

15. SINGLE CHANT.

16. SINGLE CHANT.

BENEDICTUS. St. Luke i. 68.

1. Blessed be the Lord God .... of | Is - ra- | el:
2. And hath raised up a mighty sal - - - - - - - | va - tion | for us;
3. As he spake by the mouth of his .... | Ho - ly | Prophets:
4. That we should be saved .... | from our | enemies:
5. Glory be to the Father, ... | and to the | Son:
6. As it was in the beginning, is now, ... and | ev - er | shall be:

17. DOUBLE CHANT.

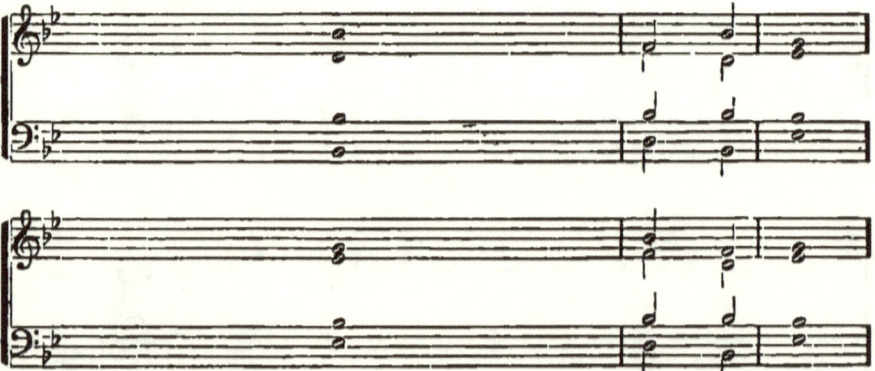

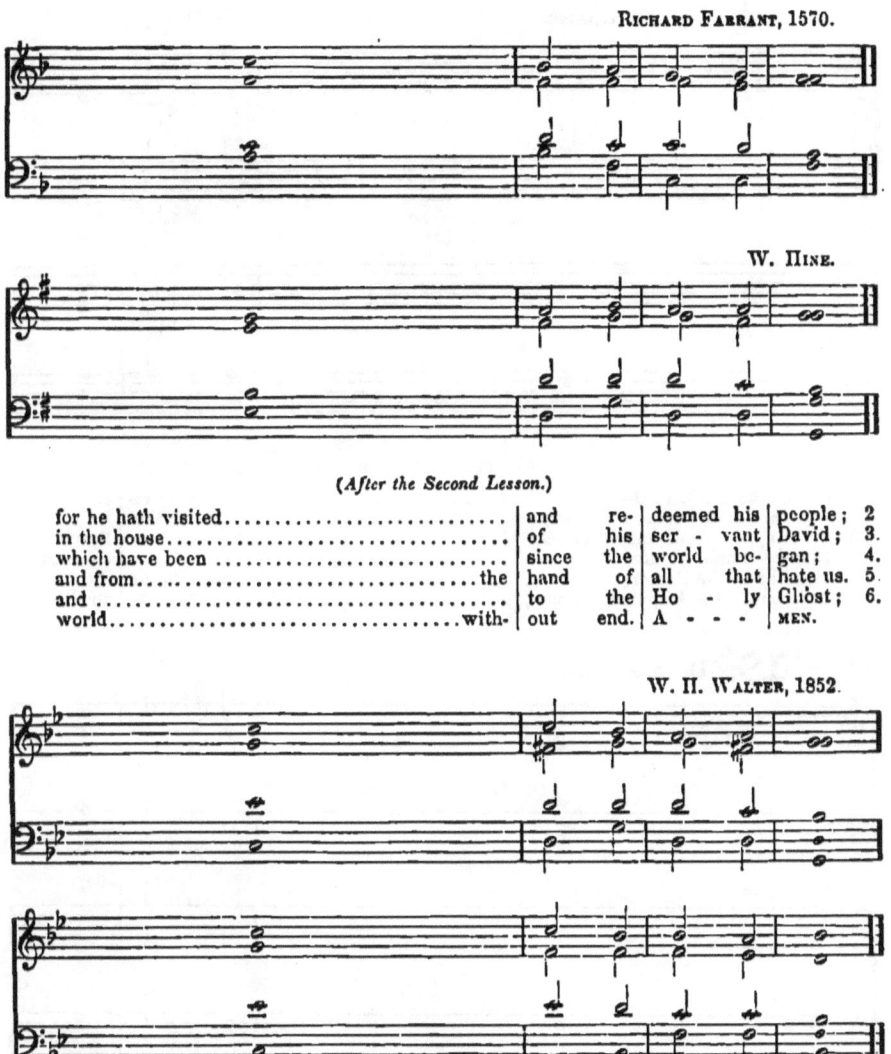

Morning Prayer.

18. Double Chant.

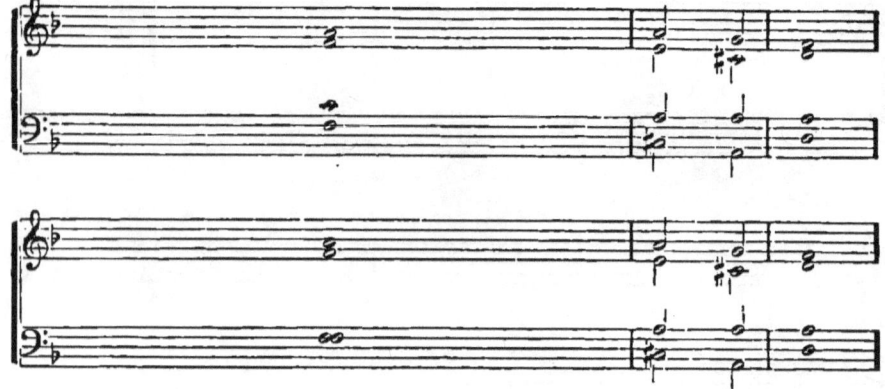

BENEDICTUS. St. Luke i. 68.

1. Blessed be the Lord God..................................of | Is - ra-| el :
2. And hath raised up a mighty sal - - - - - - va - tion | for us,
3. As he spake by the mouth of his........................| Ho - ly | Prophets,
4. That we should be saved...................................| from our | enemies,
5. Glory be to the Father,......................................| and to the | Son,
6. As it was in the beginning, is now,.....................and | ev - er | shall be,

19. Double Chant.

Evening Prayer.

20. DOUBLE CHANT.

CANTATE DOMINO. Psalm cxviii.

1. O sing unto ....the	Lord a new	song:
2. With his own right hand, and with .... his	ho - - ly	arm :
3. The Lord declared	his sal-	vation :
4. He hath remembered his mercy and truth toward the house of	Is - ra-	el :
5. Show yourselves joyful unto the Lord, ...	all ye	lands:
6. Praise the Lord .... up-	on the	harp :
7. With trumpets	also and	shawms:
8. Let the sea make a noise, and all ....that	there - in	is :
9. Let the floods clap their hands, and let the hills be joyful together } be-	fore the	Lord :
10. With righteousness shall ....ho	judge the	world :
11. Glory be to the Father	and to the	Son :
12. As it was in the beginning, is now, ...and	ev - - er	shall be.

21. DOUBLE CHANT

Evening Prayer.

Dr. Randall.

(After the First Lesson.)

for...	he hath done	marvel-lous	things.	2.
hath ....he	gotten him-	self the	victory.	3.
his righteousness hath he openly shewed	in the	sight of the	heathen.	4.
and all the ends of the world have seen the sal -	va - tion	of our	God.	5.
sing,..................................... re-	joice, and	give	thanks.	6.
sing to the harp with ....a	psalm of	thanks - -	giving.	7.
O show yourselves joyful ....be-	fore the	Lord, the	King.	8.
the round world, ... and	they that	dwell there-	in.	9.
for...	he cometh to	judge the	earth.	10.
and ....the	peo - ple	with	equity.	11.
and	to the	Ho - ly	Ghost.	12.
world ....with-	out end.	A - - -	men.	

Lord Mornington.

Evening Prayer.

22. DOUBLE CHANT.

CANTATE DOMINO. Psalm cxviii.

1. O sing unto ....the	Lord a	new	song:
2. With his own right hand, and with .... his	ho - -	ly	arm :
3. The Lord declared	his	sal-	vation :
4. He hath remembered his mercy and truth toward the house of	Is	- ra-	el :
5. Show yourselves joyful unto the Lord, ...	all	ye	lands :
6. Praise the Lord .... up-	on	the	harp :
7. With trumpets	also	and	shawms :
8. Let the sea make a noise, and all ....that	there	- in	is :
9. Let the floods clap their hands, and let the hills be joyful together } be-	fore	the	Lord :
10. With righteousness shall ....he	judge	the	world :
11. Glory be to the Father	and	to the	Son :
12. As it was in the beginning, is now,..... ....and	ev - -	er	shall be.

23. DOUBLE CHANT.

Evening Prayer.

24. Double Chant.

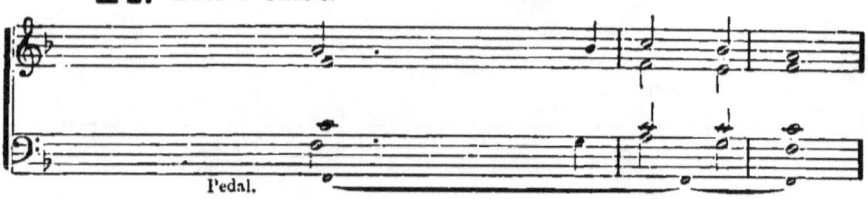

Pedal.

BONUM EST CONFITERI. Psalm xcii.

1. It is a good thing to give thanks .... un- | to   the | Lord:
2. To tell of thy loving-kindness ear -   -   -   -   ly | in   the | morning:
3. Upon an instrument of ten strings, and .... up- | on   the | lute:
4. For thou, Lord, hast made me glad...................... | through   thy | works:
5. Glory be to the Father, ... | and   to the | Son:
6. As it was in the beginning, is now,... ....and | ev   -   er | shall be:

25. Double Chant.

Evening Prayer.

(After the First Lesson.)

and to sing praises unto thy	Name,	O	Most	Highest; 2.
and of thy	truth in the	night	season; 3.
upon a loud instrument, ...	and	up-	on the	harp. 4.
and I will rejoice in giving praise for the oper -	a - tions	of	thy	hands. 5.
and	to	the	Ho - ly	Ghost; 6.
world ....with-	out	end.	A - - -	MEN.

From HANDEL.

Evening Prayer.

26. Double Chant.

BONUM EST CONFITERI. Psalm xcii.

1. It is a good thing to give thanks .... un- | to   the | Lord:
2. To tell of thy loving-kindness ear   .   -   -   ly | in   the | morning:
3. Upon an instrument of ten strings, and .... up- | on   the | lute:
4. For thou, Lord, hast made me glad............................ | through   thy | works:
5. Glory be to the Father, ... | and   to the | Son:
6. As it was in the beginning, is now,... ....and | ev -   er | shall be:

27. Double Chant.

Evening Prayer.

Dr. HODGES.

(After the First Lesson.)

and to sing praises unto thy...............	Name, O	Most	Highest; 2.
and of thy...............................	truth in the	night	season; 3.
upon a loud instrument,...................	and up-	on the	harp. 4.
and I will rejoice in giving praise for the oper -	a - tions	of thy	hands. 5.
and.....................................	to the	Ho - ly	Ghost; 6.
world ....with-	out end.	A - - -	MEN.

Dr. DUPUIS.

Evening Prayer.

28. Double Chant.

DEUS MISEREATUR. Psalm lxvii.

1. God be merciful un . . . . to | us   and | bless us:
2. That thy way may . . . . be | known   upon | earth:
3. Let the people praise . . . . | thee,   O | God:
4. O let the nations rejoice . . . . | and   be | glad:

5. Let the people praise . . . . | thee,   O | God:
6. Then shall the earth . . . . bring | forth   her | increase:
*7. God . . . . | . . . . . . shall | bless us:
8. Glory be to the Father, ... | and   to the | Son:
9. As it was in the beginning, is now, ... and | ev   -   er | shall be:

29. Double Chant.

* When a Double Chant is used, the seventh verse should be sung to the last half of the Chant.

Evening Prayer.

Christopher Teesdale.

(After the Second Lesson.)

and show us the light of his countenance, and be	merci - ful	un - to	us;	2.
thy saving	health a-	mong all	nations.	3.
yea, ...let	all the	peo - ple	praise thee.	4.
for thou shalt judge the folk righteously, and govern ....the	na - tions	up - on	earth.	5.
yea, ...let	all the	peo - ple	praise thee.	6.
and God, even our own.	God, shall	give us his	blessing.	7.
and all the ends of......................the	world shall	fear	him.	8.
and	to the	Ho - ly	Ghost;	9.
world ....with-	out end.	A - - -	MEN.	

W. H. WALTER, 1854.

Evening Prayer.

30. DOUBLE CHANT.

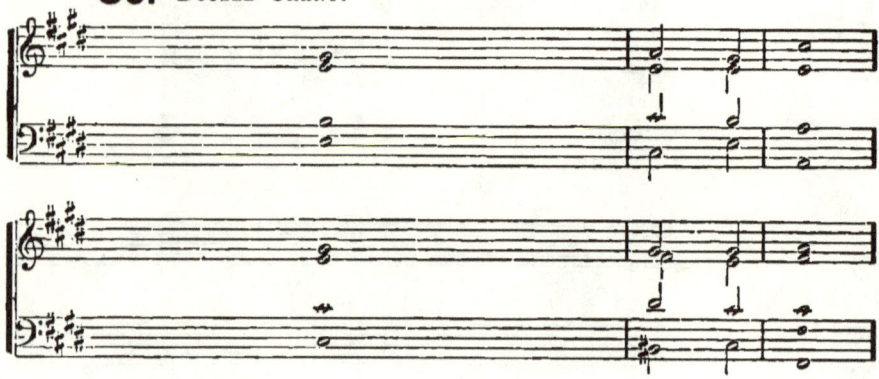

DEUS MISEREATUR. Psalm lxvii.

1. God be merciful un — — — — — — to	us	and	bless us :
2. That thy way may .... be	known	upon	earth :
3. Let the people praise	thee,	O	God :
4. O let the nations rejoice	and	be	glad :
5. Let the people praise	thee,	O	God :
6. Then shall the earth .... bring	forth	her	increase :
*7. God	......	shall	bless us :
8. Glory be to the Father, ...	and	to the	Son :
9. As it was in the beginning, is now, ... and	ev	- er	shall be :

31. DOUBLE CHANT.

* When a Double Chant is used, the seventh verse should be sung to the last half of the Chant.

Evening Prayer.

W. H. Walter, 1850.

(After the Second Lesson.)

and show us the light of his countenance, and be	merci - ful	un - to	us;	2.
thy saving .... health	a- mong	all	nations.	3.
yea, ... let	all the	peo - ple	praise thee.	4.
for thou shalt judge the folk righteously, and govern .... the	na - tions	up - on	earth.	5.
yea, ... let	all the	peo - ple	praise thee.	6.
and God, even our own	God, shall	give us his	blessing.	7.
and all the ends of .... the	world shall	fear	him.	8.
and .... to	the	Ho - ly	Ghost;	9
world .... with-	out end.	A - -	MEN.	

W. H. Walter, 1850.

Evening Prayer

32. Double Chant.

BENEDIC, ANIMA MEA. Psalm ciii.

1. Praise the LORD, ...	O	my	soul:
2. Praise the LORD, ...	O	my	soul:
3. Who forgiveth	all	thy	sin:
4. Who saveth thy life	from	de-	struction:
5. O praise the LORD, ye Angels of his, ye that .... ex-	cel	in	strength:
6. O praise the LORD,..all	ye	his	hosts:
*7. O speak good of the LORD, all ye works of his, in all places ..of	his	do-	minion:
8. Glory be to the Father, ...	and	to the	Son;
9. As it was in the beginning, is now, ...and	ev	- er	shall be

33. Double Chant.

* The seventh verse, "O speak good," &c., should be sung to the last half of a Double Chant.

Evening Prayer.

JOHN NORRIS.

(After the Second Lesson.)

and all that is within me, ...	praise his	ho - ly	Name.	2.
and .... for-	get not	all his	benefits;	3.
and	heal - eth	all thine in-	firmities;	4.
and crowneth thee .... with	mercy and	lov - ing-	kindness.	5.
ye that fulfil his commandment, and hearken unto the	voice of	his	word.	6.
ye servants .... of	his that	do his	pleasure.	7.
praise thou .... the	Lord, ...	O my	soul.	8.
and	to the	Ho - ly	Ghost;	9.
world .... with-	out end.	A - - -	MEN.	

Evening Prayer.

34. Double Chant.

BENEDIC, ANIMA MEA. Psalm ciii.

```
1. Praise the LORD, ............................................. | O        my | soul :
2. Praise the LORD, ............................................. | O        my | soul :
3. Who forgiveth ................................................ | all      thy | sin :
4. Who saveth thy life .......................................... from de- | struction :
5. O praise the LORD, ye Angels of his, ye that ............... ex- | cel       in | strength :
6. O praise the LORD, ........................................ all | ye       his | hosts :
*7. O speak good of the LORD, all ye works of his, in all places ..of | his       do- | minion :
8. Glory be to the Father, ...................................... | and   to the | Son :
9. As it was in the beginning, is now, ......................... and | ev    -   er | shall be :
```

35. Double Chant.

* The seventh verse, "*O speak good,*" &c., should be sung to the last half of a Double Chant.

 Easter Day. (Morning Prayer.)

36. DOUBLE CHANT.

(Instead of the Psalm, "O come, let us sing," &c.)

1. Christ our Passover,..is | sacri - ficed | for us :
2. Not with the old leaven, neither with the leaven ....of | malice and | wickedness:
3. Christ being raised from the dead,.......................... | dieth no | more :
4. For in that he died, he died un - - - - - to | sin .... | once :
5. Likewise reckon ye also yourselves to be dead indeed .... | un to | sin :
6. Christ is risen.. | from the | dead :
7. For since .... by | man came | death :
8. For as ....in | Adam all | die :
9. Glory be to the Father .... | and to the | Son:
10. As it was in the beginning, is now, ...and | ev - - er | shall be :

37. SINGLE CHANT.

38. SINGLE CHANT

Thanksgiving Day. (Morning Prayer.)

39. Double Chant.

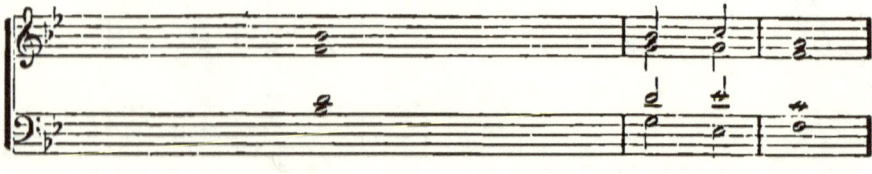

(*Instead of* "O come, let us sing," &c.)

1. Praise ye the Lord; for it is good to sing praises .... | unto   our | God:
2. The Lord doth build up .... Je- | ru -   sa- | lem:
3. He healeth those that are .... | broken   in | heart:
4. He covereth the heaven with clouds, and prepareth .... | rain   for the | earth:
5. He giveth to .... the | beast   his | food:
6. Praise the Lord, ... | O   Je- | rusalem:
7. For he hath strengthened .... the | bars of   thy | gates:
8. He maketh peace .... | in   thy | borders:
9. Glory be to the Father, ... | and   to the | Son:
10. As it was in the beginning, is now, ... and | ev -   er | shall be:

40. Single Chant.

41. Single Chant.

Thanksgiving Day. *(Morning Prayer.)* 43

W. H. WALTER, 1853.

for it is	pleasant and	praise is	comely. 2.
he gathereth together .... the	out-casts of	Is - ra-	el. 3.
and	bind - eth	up their	wounds. 4.
he maketh the grass .... to	grow up-	on the	mountains 5.
and to .... the	young......	ravens which	cry. 6.
praise	...... thy	God, O	Sion. 7.
he hath	blessed thy	children with-	in thee. 8.
and filleth thee with .... the	fin - est	of the	wheat. 9.
and	to the	Ho - ly	Ghost; 10.
world .... with-	out end.	A - - -	MEN.

V. NOVELLO.

PETER FUSSELL.

Burial of the Dead.

42. Double Chant.

1. Lord, let me know my end, and the number .... of | my | days:
3. For man walketh in a vain shadow, and disquieteth ...... him- | self | in | vain:
5. Deliver me from all .... | mine | of- | fences:
7. Hear my prayer, O Lord, and with thine ears .... con- | sider | my | calling:
9. O spare me a little, that I may .... re- | cover | my | strength:
11. Before the mountains were brought forth, or ever the earth ..... and the | world | were | made:
13. For a thousand years in thy sight .... are | but | as | yesterday:
15. In the morning it is green, ... and | grow - | eth | up:
17. Thou hast set our .... mis- | deeds | be- | fore thee:
19. The days of our age are threescore years and ten; and though men be so strong that they come .... to | four - | score | years:
21. Glory be to the Father, ... | and | to the | Son:

2. Behold, thou hast made my days as it were a span long, and mine age is even as nothing in .... re- | spect | of | thee:
4. And now, Lord, ... | what is | my | hope:
6. When thou with rebukes doth chasten man for sin, thou makest his beauty to consume away, like as it were a moth .... | fretting | a | garment:
8. For I am .... a | stranger with | thee:
10. Lord, thou hast .... | been | our | refuge:
12. Thou turnest man .... | to | de- | struction:
14. As soon as thou scatterest them they are even .... | as | a | sleep:
16. For we consume away .... in | thy | dis- | pleasure:
18. For when thou art angry, all .... our | days | are | gone:
20. So teach us .... to | number | our | days:
22. As it was in the beginning, is now, ... and | ev - | er | shall be:

43. Single Chant.

Double Chants.

44. Gloria Patri.

45. Benedicite.

46.

47.

Double Chants.

J. Jones.

W. H. Walter, 1856.

Dr. Dupuis.

John Soaper.

Double Chants.

Double Chants.

Dr. Dupuis.

Isaac Barrow.

W. H. Walter, 1855.

Wm. Russell.

Double Chants.

52.

53.

54.

55.

Double Chants.

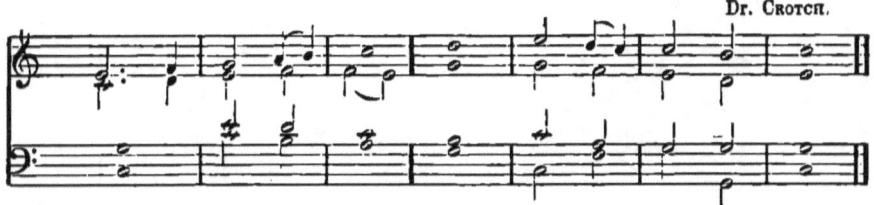
Dr. Crotch.

W. H. Walter, 1851.

Edward Higgins.

Double Chants.

56. Te Deum.

57.

58.

59. Minor.

Double Chants.

Theo. H. Smith.

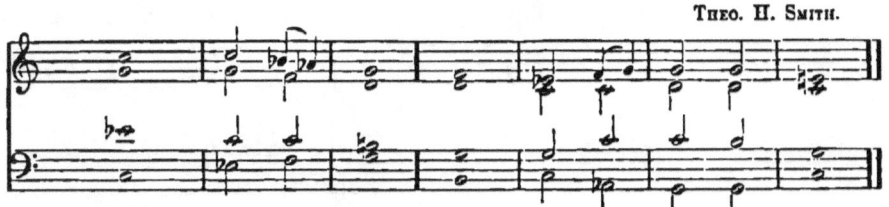

W. H. Walter, 1859.

Dr. Hodges.

James Flintoft.

Single Chants.

60. V. NOVELLO.

61. W. H. WALTER, 1848.

62. W. RUSSELL.

63.

Single Chants.

64. T. Purcell.

65. Dr. W. Hayes.

66. V. Novello.

67. Travers.

Single Chants.

68. Minor. — Dr. Blow, 1675.

69. Minor. — Farrant.

70. — Dr. Arnold.

71. — W. H. Walter, 1854.

Single Chants.

72. Rev. Wm. Tucker.

73. Dr. Crotch.

74. Dr. Ayrton.

75. Minor. W. H. Walter, 1854.

Single Chants.

76. W. Russell.

77. J. Travers.

78. Dr. Turner.

79. Rev. Wm. Felton.

Single Chants.

80. Dr. Crotch.

81. Dr. Dupuis.

82. Wm. Russell.

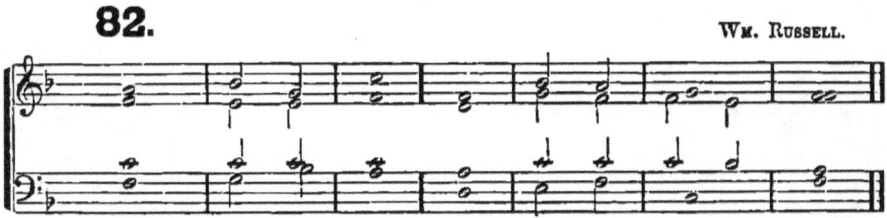

83. The Grand Chant. Pelham Humphrey.

Kyrie Eleison.
(At the Decalogue.)

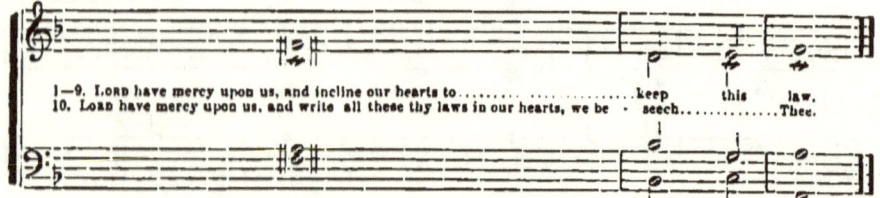

Gloria tibi, Domine.
(Before the Gospel.)

Sanctus.
(After "Therefore with Angels," &c.)

PSALM AND HYMN TUNES.

ABBEY. C. M.

1. RAVENSCROFT. 1621.

Thus God declares his sov'reign will: "The King that I ordain, Whose throne is fix'd on Sion's hill, Shall there securely reign."

BRAINTREE. C. M.

BRISTOL. C. M.
Dr. Hodges.

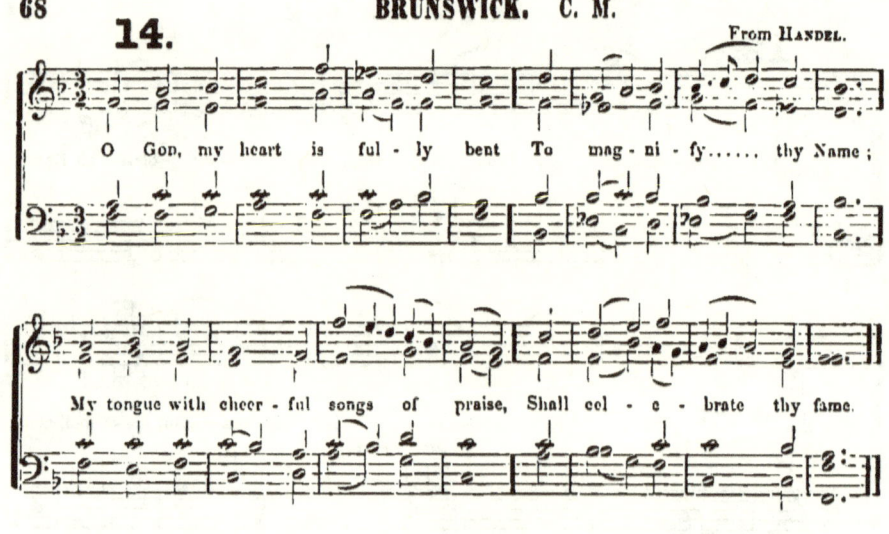

CHESTNUT RIDGE. C. M.

20.

W. H. Walter. 1860.

There is a land of pure de-light, Where saints im-mor-tal reign;
E-ter-nal day ex-cludes the night, And pleas-ures ban-ish pain.

CHICHESTER. C. M.

21.

J. Ravenscroft. 1621.

For-ev-er and for-ev-er, Lord, Unchang'd thou dost re-main;
Thy word, es-tab-lish'd in the heav'ns, Does all their orbs sus-tain

CHRISTMAS. C. M.

From HANDEL.

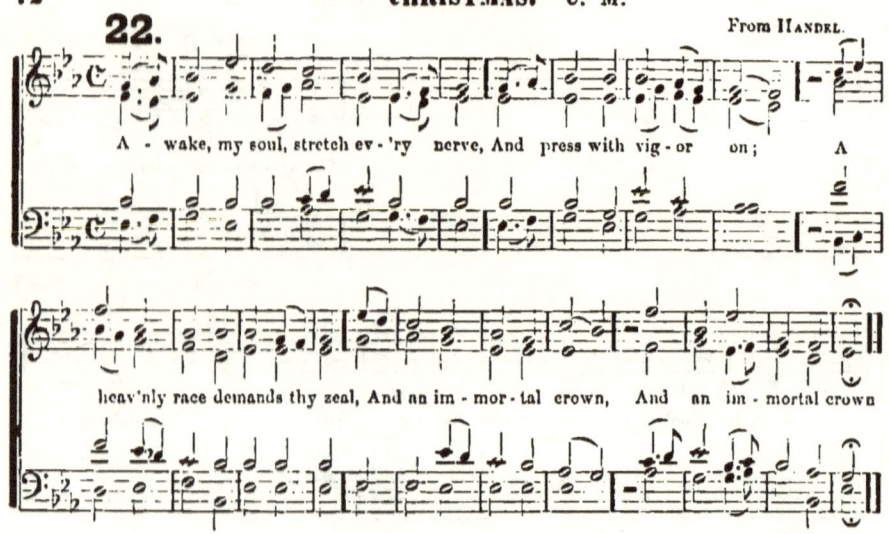

A-wake, my soul, stretch ev-'ry nerve, And press with vig-or on; A heav'nly race demands thy zeal, And an im-mor-tal crown, And an im-mortal crown

CHRIST'S HOSPITAL. C. M.

O let tri-umph-ant faith dis-pel The fears of guilt and woe; If God be for us, God the LORD, Who, who shall be our foe!

COLCHESTER. C. M.
A. WILLIAMS.

COVENTRY. C. M.

DANTZIC. C. M.

26.

Say ye, the Lord shall not regard, Shall not your sins discern?

Take heed, ye foolish and unwise; When will you wisdom learn?

DUMFERLINE. C. M.

27.

Thos. Tomkins. *Mus. Bac.* 1620.

The spacious earth is all the Lord's, The Lord's her fulness is;

The world, and they that dwell therein, By sov'reign right are his.

LONDON. C. M. 79

36.

Dr. Croft.

Thou, God, all glo-ry, hon-our, pow'r, Art wor-thy to re-ceive;

Since all things by thy pow'r were made, And by thy boun-ty live.

LUTZEN. C. M.

37.

Nicholas Hermann. 1560.

To God, our nev-er-fail-ing strength, With loud ap-plaus-es sing;

And joint-ly make a cheer-ful noise To Ja-cob's aw-ful King

MANCHESTER. C. M.
Dr. Wainright, (of England.)

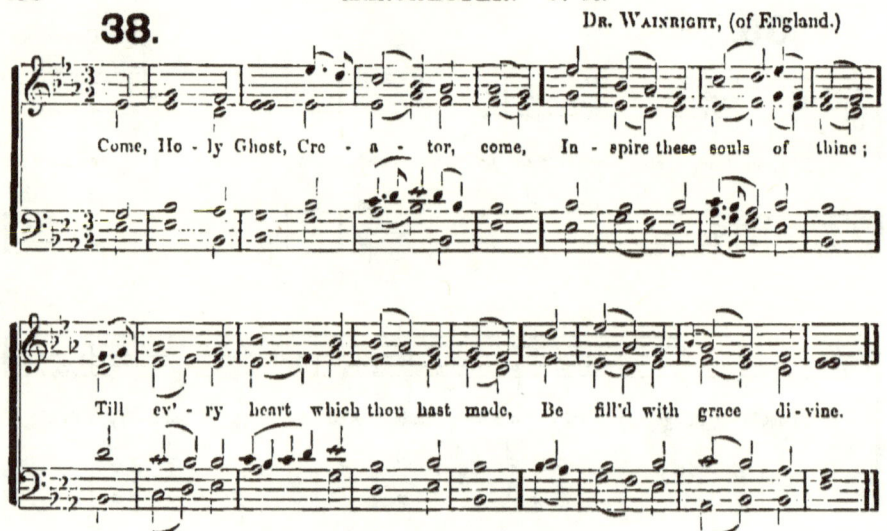

MARTYRDOM. C. M.
R. Gamble.

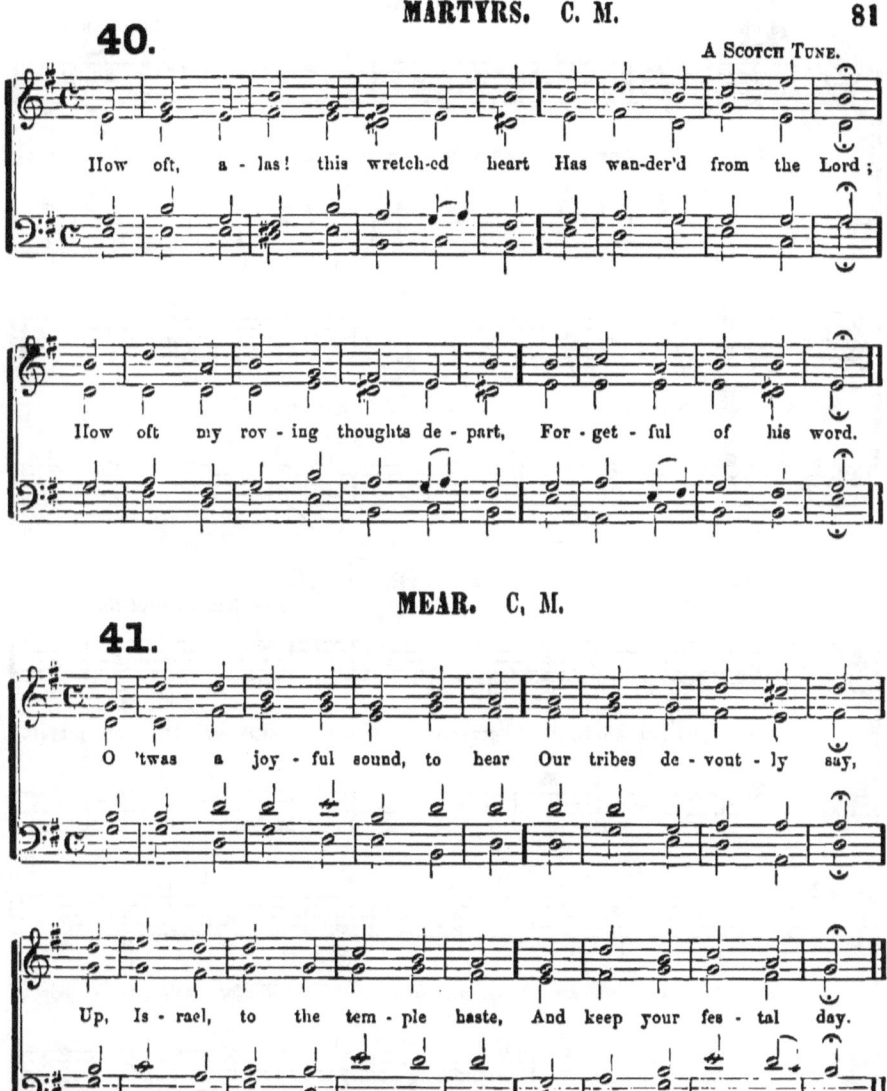

NORTON. C. M.

44. Arranged from HANDEL.

How good and plea-sant must it be To thank the LORD most high;
And with re-peat-ed hymns of praise His Name to mag-ni--fy!

OLD ENGLISH TUNE. C. M.

45. GIBBONS.

O thou, to whom all crea-tures bow With-in this earth-ly frame,
Through all the world how great art thou! How glo-rious is thy Name!

REDEMPTION. C. M.

46. W. H. Walter, 1859.

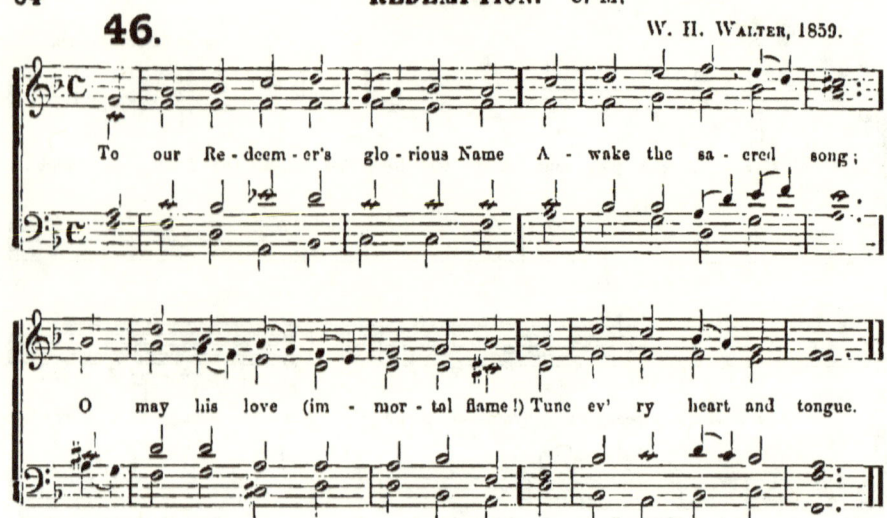

To our Redeemer's glorious Name Awake the sacred song;
O may his love (immortal flame!) Tune ev'ry heart and tongue.

SALISBURY. (Old.) C. M.

47. T. Ravenscroft.

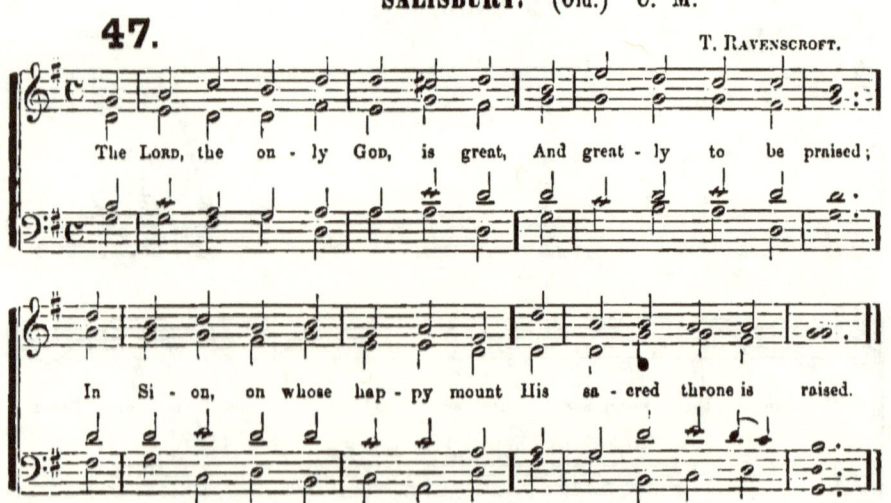

The Lord, the only God, is great, And greatly to be praised;
In Sion, on whose happy mount His sacred throne is raised.

48. Dr. C. Burney.

Let heaven a-rise, let earth ap-pear, Pro-claim'd th' E-ter-nal Lord:
The heaven a-rose, the earth ap-pear'd, At his.... cre-a-ting word.

ST. ALBANS. C. M.

49. W. H. Walter, 1849.

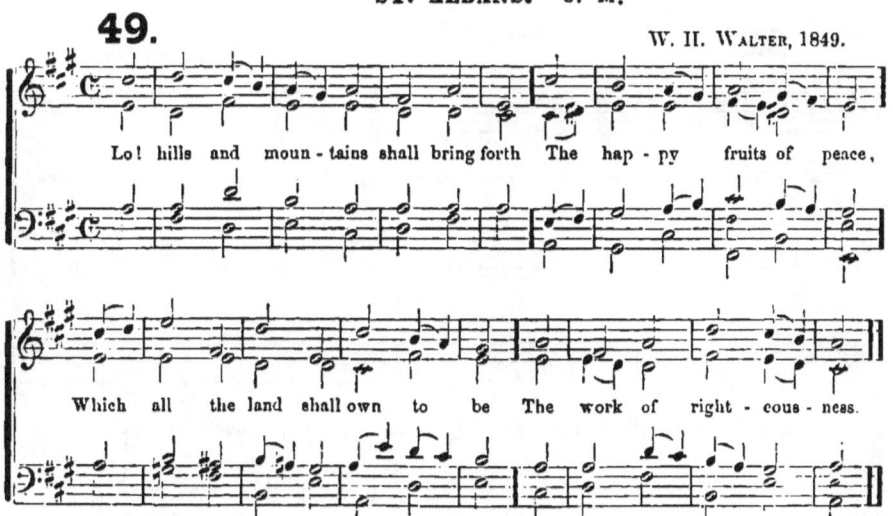

Lo! hills and moun-tains shall bring forth The hap-py fruits of peace,
Which all the land shall own to be The work of right-cous-ness.

50. ST. ANN'S. C. M.
Dr. Croft.

Thou art the Way, to thee a-lone From sin and death we flee;
And he who would the Father seek, Must seek him, Lord, by thee.

51. ST. ELISABETH. C. M.
W. H. Walter, 1848.

Sing to the Lord a new-made song, Who wondrous things has done;
With his right hand and holy arm, The conquest he has won

ST. JAMES. C. M.

52. R. Courtville.

How blest are they who always keep The pure and perfect way;
Who never from the sacred paths Of God's commandments stray.

ST. LUKE'S. C. M.

53. W. H. Walter. 1848.

When all thy mercies, O my God, My rising soul surveys,
Transported with the view, I'm lost, In wonder, love, and praise!

54. ST. MAGNUS. (or Nottingham.) C. M.
Dr. Jer. Clark.

In-struct me in thy stat-utes, Lord, Thy righteous paths dis-play;

And I, from them, through all my life, Will nev-er go a-stray.

55. ST. MARY'S. C. M.
Dr. Blow.

Few are thy days, and full of wo, O man, of wo-man born:

Thy doom is writ-ten; "Dust thou art, To dust thou shalt re-turn."

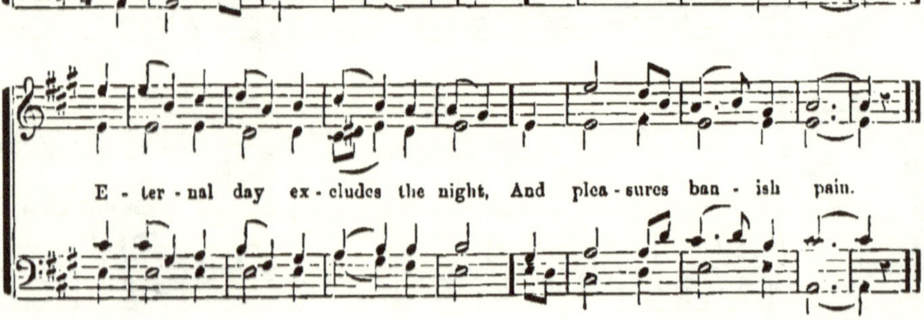

TIVERTON. C. M.

60. GRIGG.

The Lord him-self, the might-y Lord, Vouch-safes to be my guide;
The Shep-herd, by whose con-stant care, My wants are all sup-plied.

TRINITY CHAPEL. C. M.

61. W. H. WALTER, 1859.

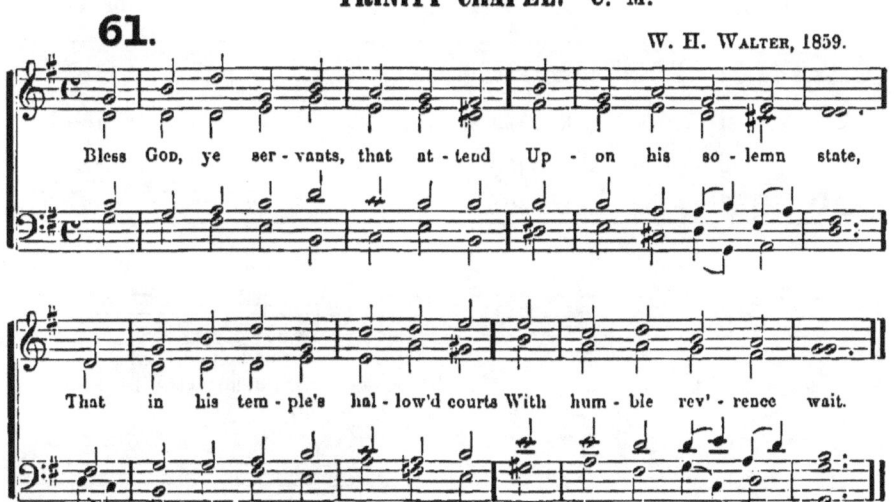

Bless God, ye ser-vants, that at-tend Up-on his so-lemn state,
That in his tem-ple's hal-low'd courts With hum-ble rev'-rence wait.

TOTTENHAM. C. M.

TYE. C. M.

Dr. Tye.

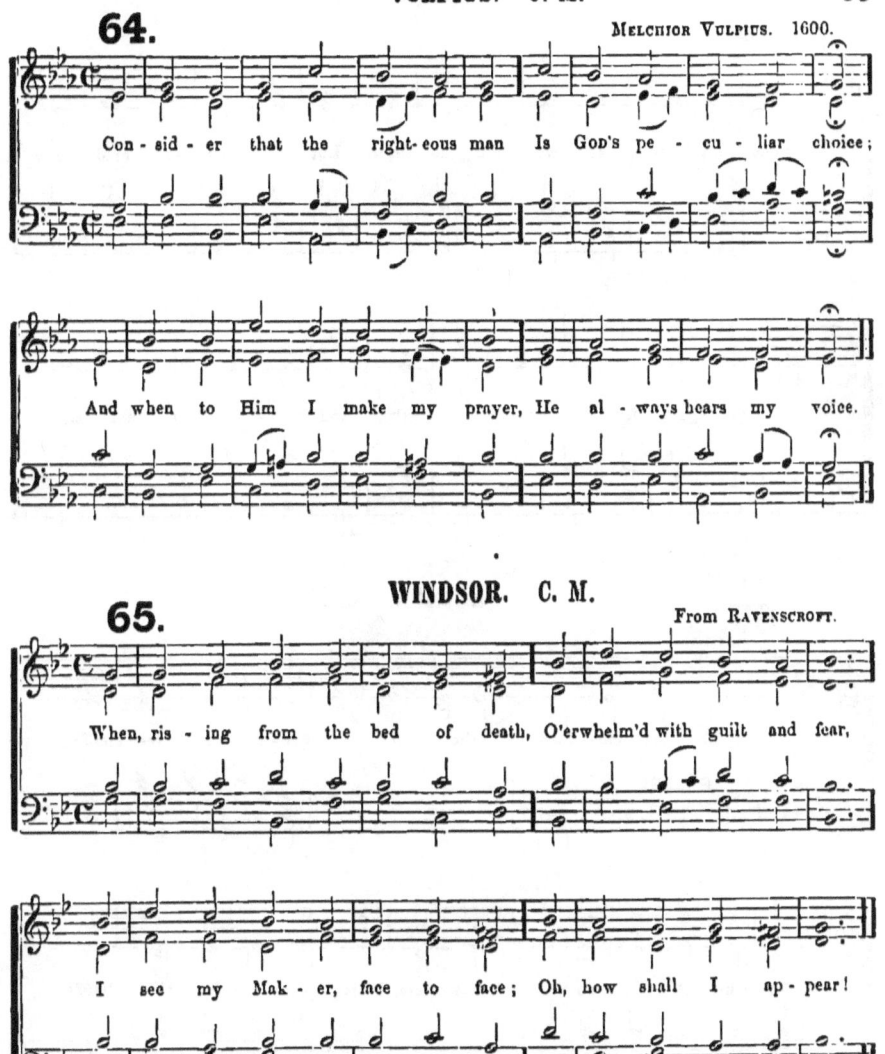

66. YORK. C. M.
JOHN MILTON.

LORD, not to us, we claim no share, But to thy sa-cred name

Give glo-ry, for thy mer-cy's sake, And truth's e-ter-nal fame.

67. ZURICH. C. M.

See, in the vine-yard of the Lord, A bar-ren fig-tree stands;

No fruit it yields, no blos-som bears, Though plant-ed by His hands.

DUNGENESS. C. M. Double.

68. Arranged from Mozart.

While beau-ty clothes the fer-tile vale, And blos-soms on the spray,

And fra-grance breathes in ev'-ry gale, How sweet the ver-nal day!

Hark! how the fea-ther'd war-blers sing! 'Tis na-ture's cheer-ful voice;

Soft mu-sic hails the love-ly spring, And woods and fields re-joice.

TOLLAND. C. M. Double.

REGINALD SPOFFORTH.

ANGEL'S HYMN. L. M.

72.

Orlando Gibbons, 1623.

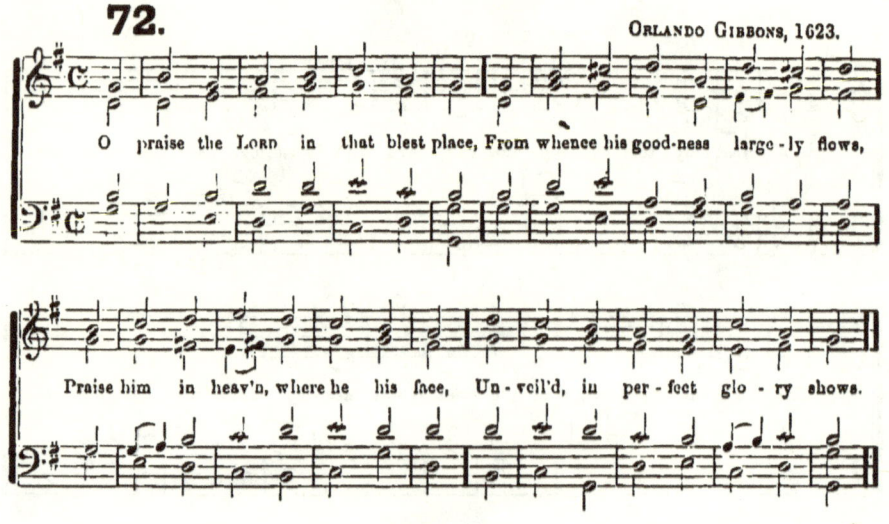

O praise the Lord in that blest place, From whence his good-ness large-ly flows,

Praise him in heav'n, where he his face, Un-veil'd, in per-fect glo-ry shows.

ASCENSION. L. M.

73.

Gibbons.

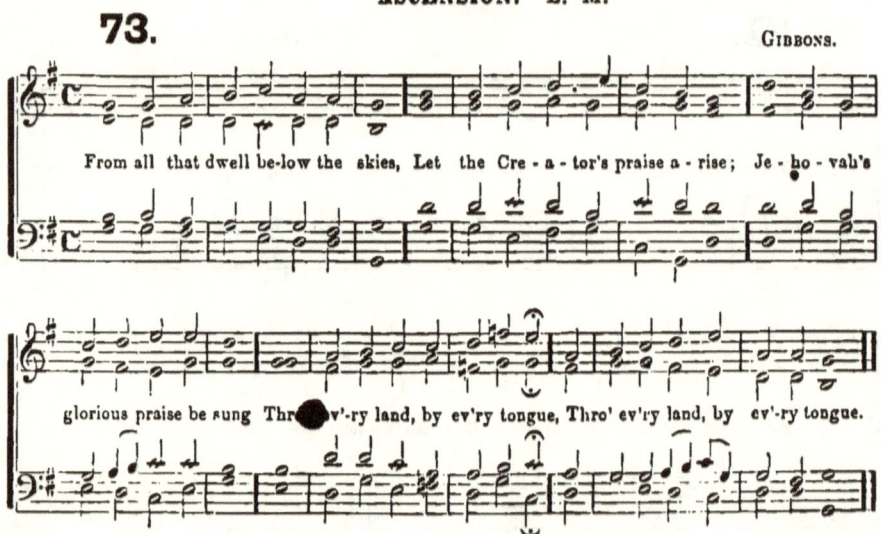

From all that dwell be-low the skies, Let the Cre-a-tor's praise a-rise; Je-ho-vah's

glorious praise be sung Thro' ev'ry land, by ev'ry tongue, Thro' ev'ry land, by ev'ry tongue.

ATLANTIC. L. M.

74. Geo. Oates.

Great God, to thee my ev'n-ing song, With humble gratitude I raise;
O let thy mercy tune my tongue, And fill my heart with lively praise.

BARTHOLDY. L. M.

75. Arranged from Mendelssohn.

All glorious God, what hymns of praise Shall our transported voices raise:
What ardent love and zeal are due, While heav'n stands open to our view.

BENEVOLENCE. L. M.

76. Dr. HODGES.

For thee, O God, our con-stant praise In Zi-on waits, thy cho-sen seat;
Our prom-is'd al-tars there we'll raise, And all our zeal-ous vows com-plete.

BERLIN. L. M.

77. GEORGE NEUMARK, 1650.

When I sur-vey the wond'-rous cross On which the Prince of Glo-ry died,
My rich-est gain I count but loss, And pour con-tempt on all my pride.

COBURG. L. M.

80.

Arranged from Luther's Choral;
"*Ein' feste Burg ist unser Gott.*"

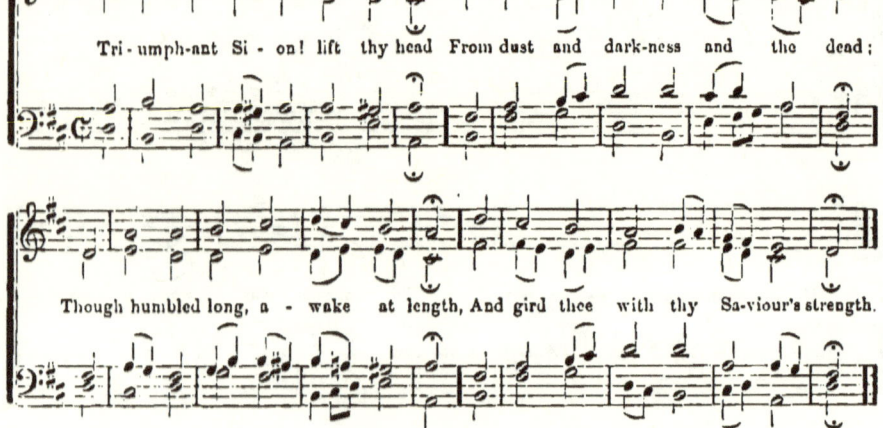

Tri-umph-ant Si-on! lift thy head From dust and dark-ness and the dead;

Though humbled long, a-wake at length, And gird thee with thy Sa-viour's strength.

DUKE STREET. L. M.

81.

J. Hatton.

God is gone up, our Lord and King, With shouts of joy, and trumpet's sound,

To him re-peat-ed prais-es sing, And let the cheer-ful song re-bound.

103

82. ELNO. L. M.

Arranged by Conrad Kocher.

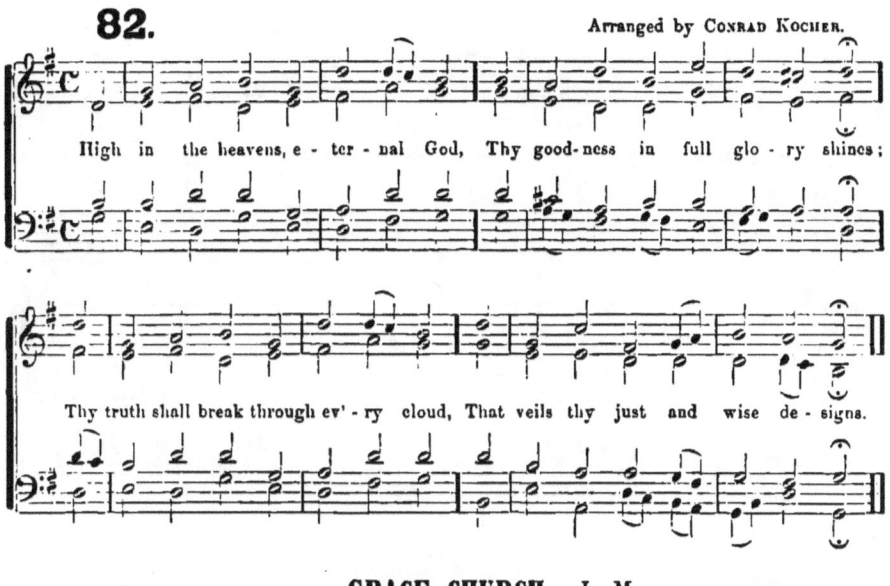

High in the heavens, e-ter-nal God, Thy good-ness in full glo-ry shines;

Thy truth shall break through ev'-ry cloud, That veils thy just and wise de-signs.

83. GRACE CHURCH. L. M.

From Pleyel.

Fa-ther of all, whose love pro-found A ran-som for our souls hath found,

Be-fore thy throne we sin-ners bend; To us thy pard'-ning love ex-tend.

MOZART. L. M.

90. From Mozart.

Let me with light and truth be bless'd; Be these my guides to lead the way,

Till on Thy ho-ly hill I rest, And in Thy sa-cred tem-ple pray.

NAZARETH. L. M.

91. S. Wedde.

O hap-py day, that stays my choice On thee, my Sa-viour and my God,

Well may this glow-ing heart re-joice, And tell thy good-ness all a-broad.

NINETY-SEVENTH PSALM TUNE. L. M.

92. TUCKEY.

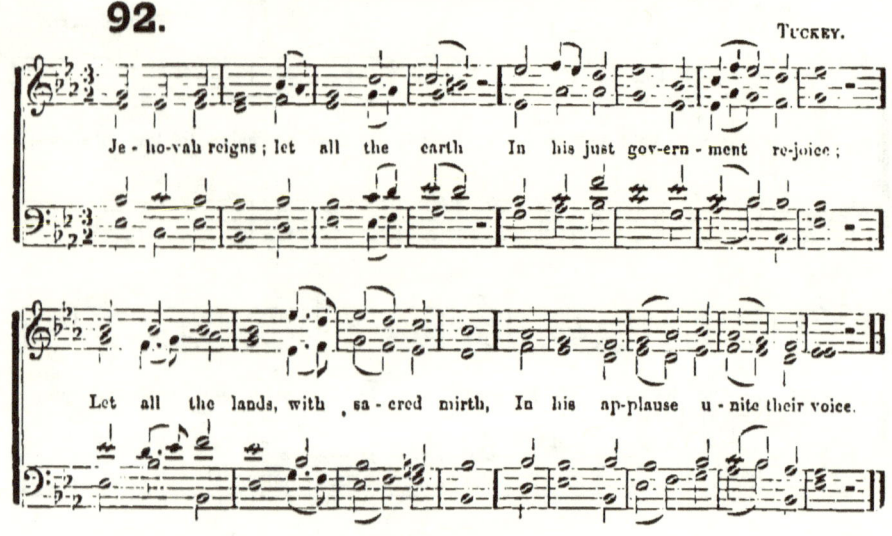

Je-ho-vah reigns; let all the earth In his just gov-ern-ment re-joice;

Let all the lands, with sa-cred mirth, In his ap-plause u-nite their voice.

OLD HUNDREDTH. L. M.

93.

With one con-sent let all the earth, To God their cheer-ful voi-ces raise;

Glad hom-age pay, with aw-ful mirth, And sing be-fore him songs of praise.

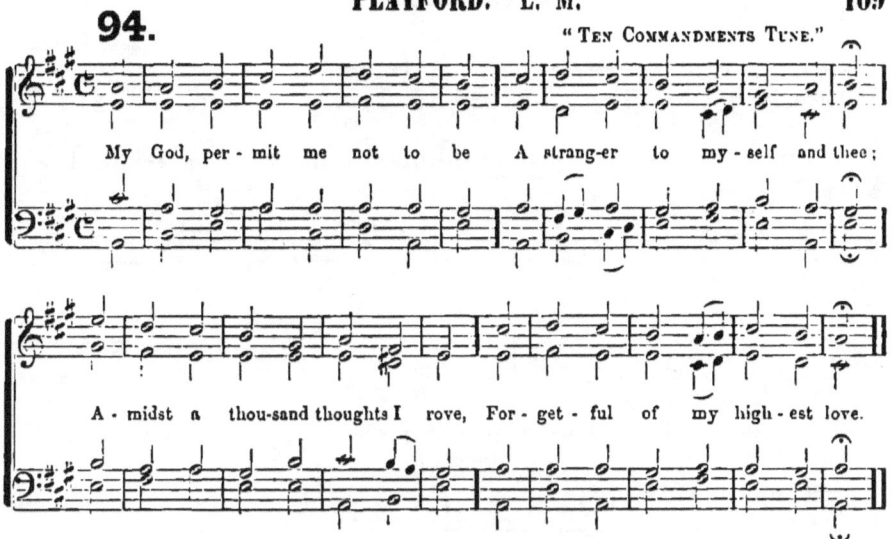

SAMSON. L. M.

98. From HANDEL.

Tri - umph - ant Si - on! lift thy head From dust, and dark-ness, and the dead:
Though humbled long, a - wake at length, And gird thee with thy Saviour's strength.

SEASONS. L. M.

99. From PLEYEL.

E - ter - nal Source of ev' - ry joy! Well may thy praise our lips em-ploy,
While in thy tem-ple we ap - pear, To hail thee, Sov'-reign of... the year.

SEBASTIAN. L. M.

100.

Melody by J. A. Johnson.
Harmony by W. H. Walter, 1846.

Ye that in might and pow'r ex-cel, Your grate-ful sa-cri-fice pre-pare;
God's glo-rious ac-tions loud-ly tell; His won-drous pow'r to all de-clare.

SPRING. L. M.

101.

From Haydn's "Creation."

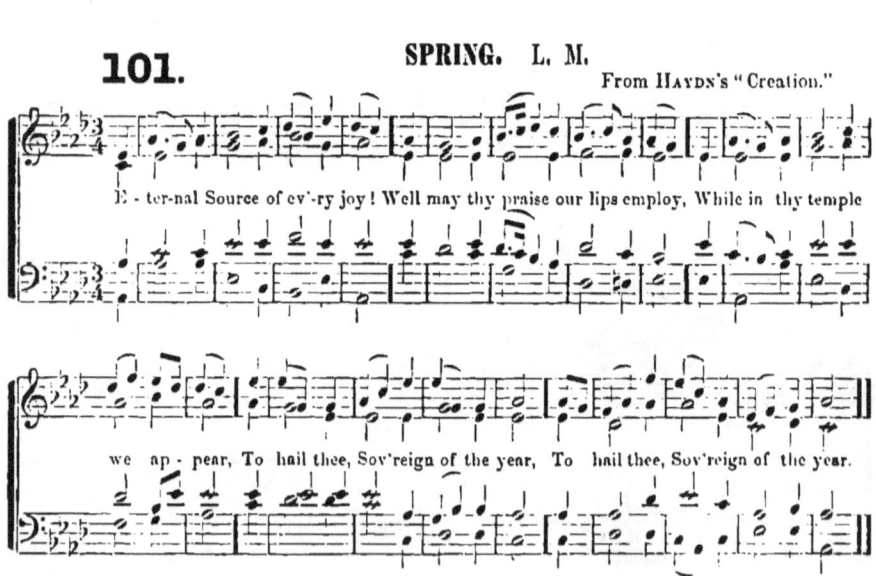

E-ter-nal Source of ev'-ry joy! Well may thy praise our lips employ, While in thy temple we ap-pear, To hail thee, Sov'reign of the year, To hail thee, Sov'reign of the year.

102. STONEFIELD. L. M.
STANLEY.

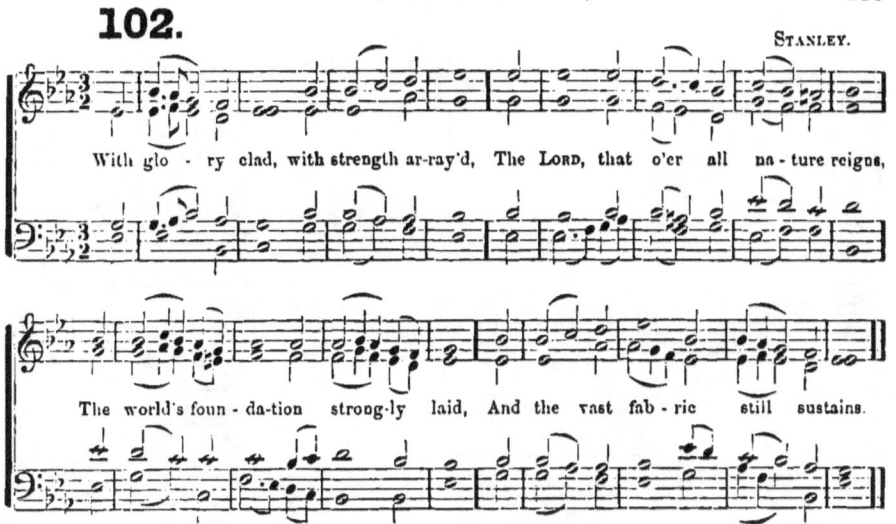

103. SURREY. L. M.
COSTELLO.

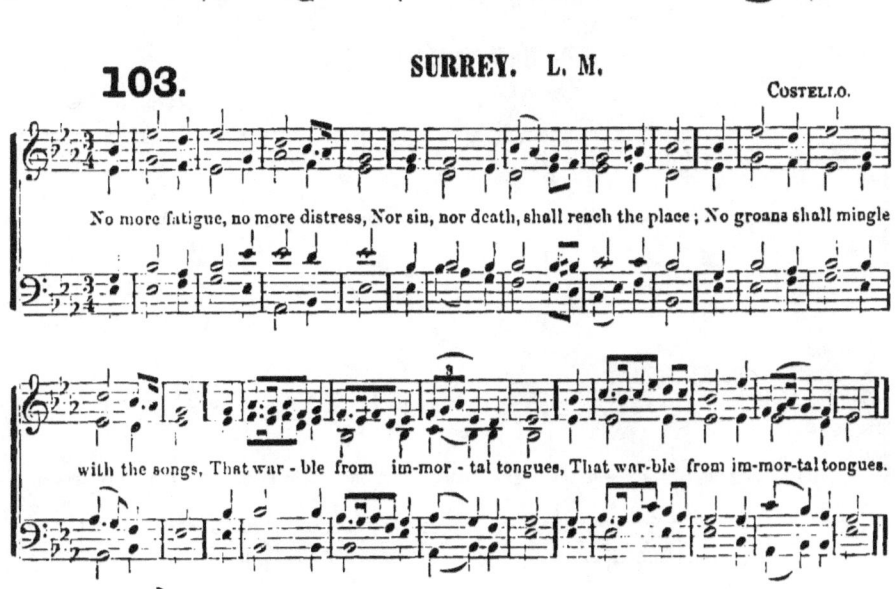

ST. AUGUSTINE. L. M.

104. From an ancient Choral.

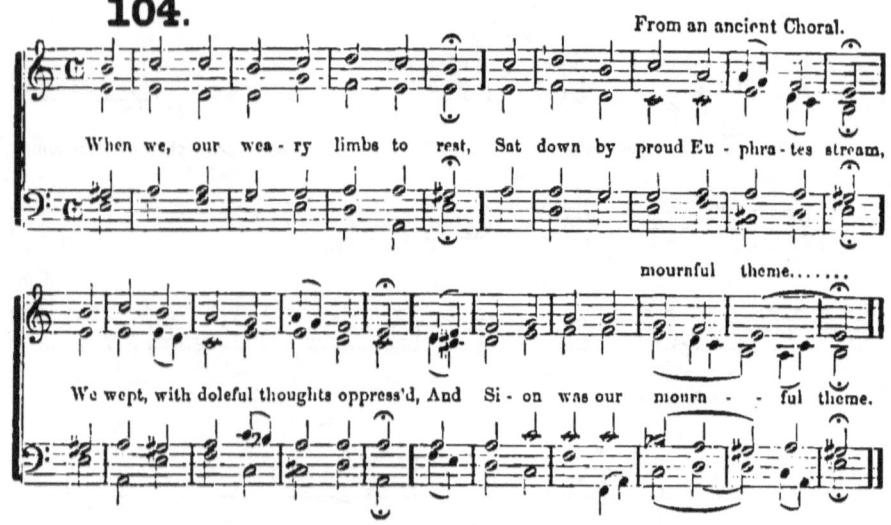

When we, our weary limbs to rest, Sat down by proud Euphrates stream,
We wept, with doleful thoughts oppress'd, And Sion was our mournful theme.

ST. BARTHOLOMEW'S. L. M.

105. From "NATIONAL LYRE."

O thou that hear'st when sinners cry, Though all my crimes before thee lie,
Behold them not with an angry look, But blot their mem'ry from thy book.

ST. BASIL. L. M.

106. W. H. Walter. 1852.

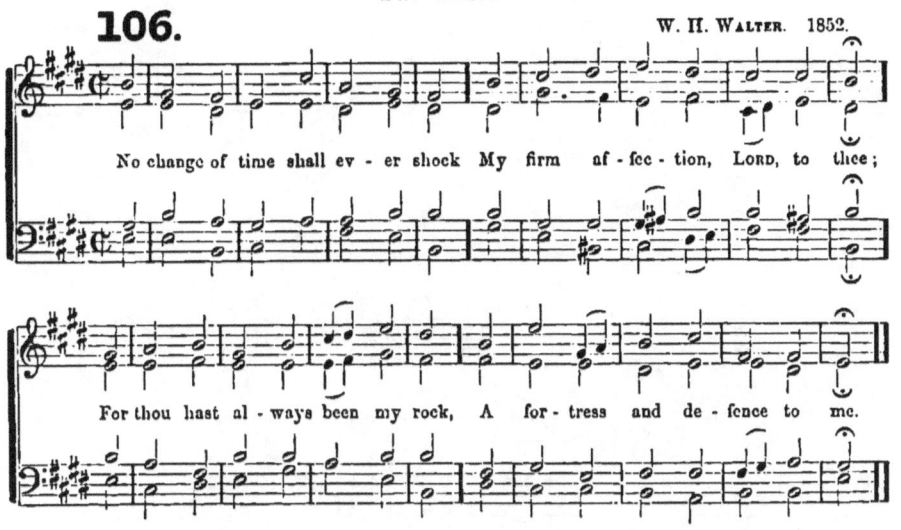

ST. CHRYSOSTOM. L. M.

107. W. H. Walter. 1852.

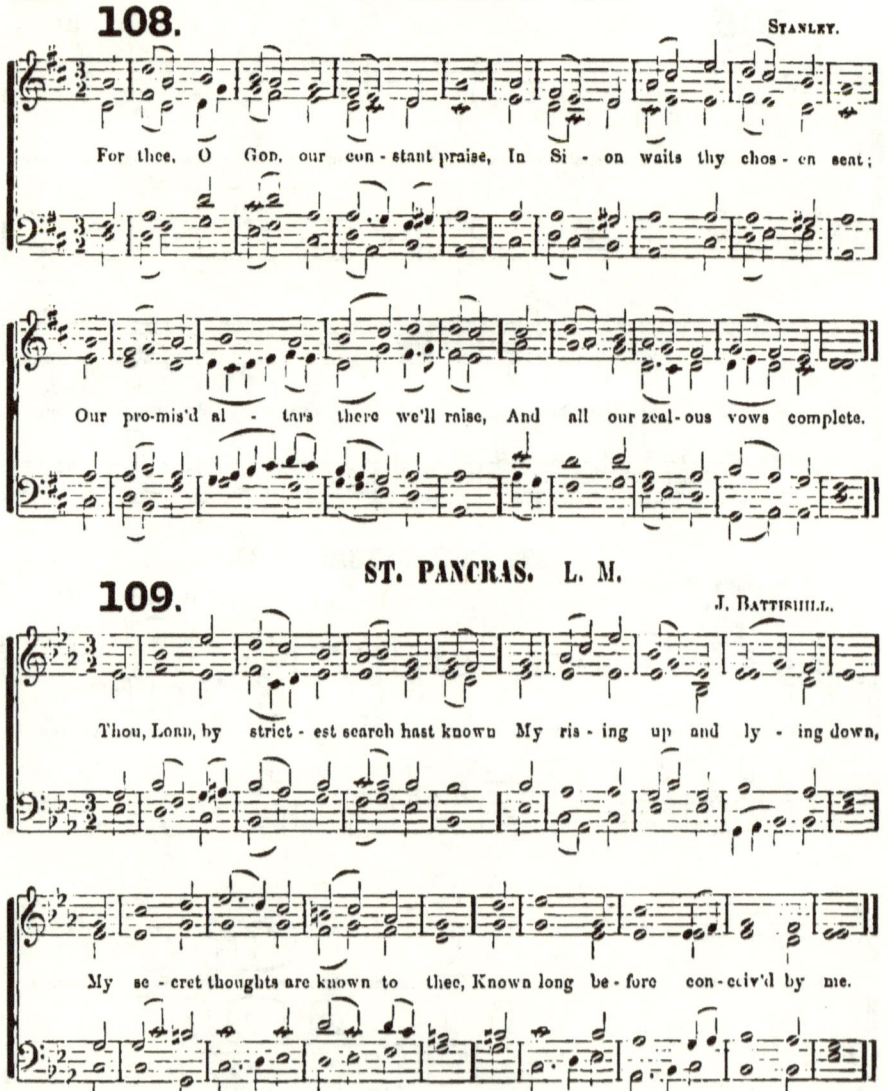

TALLIS' CANON. L. M.

112.

From Abp. Parker's Psalter. 1551.
Rev. Mr. Havergal's Version.

Praise God, from whom all blessings flow, Praise him, all creatures here below;
Praise him above, angelic host; Praise Father, Son, and Holy Ghost.

TALLIS' EVENING HYMN. L. M.

113.

A popular version of Tallis' Canon.

Glory to thee, my God, this night, For all the blessings of the light;
Keep me, O keep me, King of kings, Under thine own Almighty wings.

TOWNER. L. M.

114. W. H. Walter. 1850.

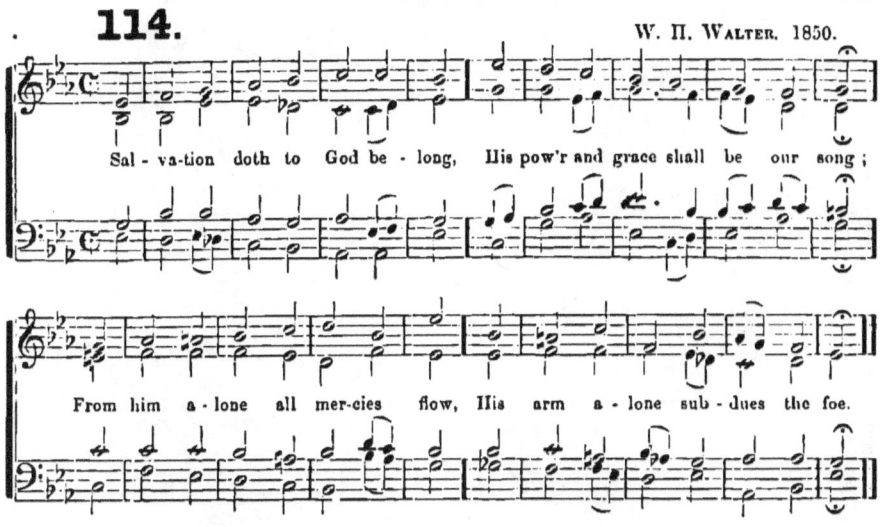

Sal-va-tion doth to God be-long, His pow'r and grace shall be our song;
From him a-lone all mer-cies flow, His arm a-lone sub-dues the foe.

TRINITY. L. M.

115. Martin Luther. 1530.

O ho-ly, ho-ly, ho-ly Lord, Bright in thy deeds, and in thy Name,
For ev-er be thy Name a-dor'd, Thy glo-ries let the world proclaim.

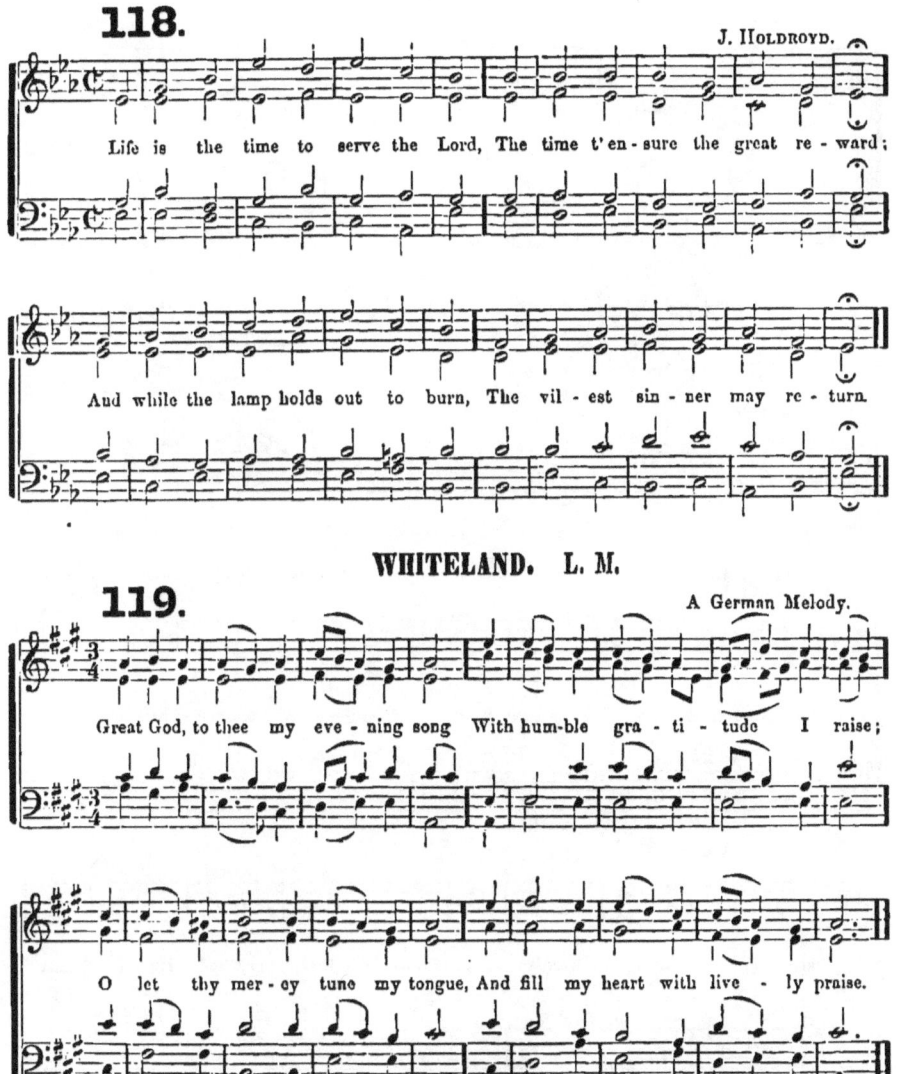

WINDHAM. L. M.

122.

Daniel Reed. 1800.

Broad is the road that leads to death, And thousands walk together there;
But wisdom shows a narrow path, With here and there a traveler.

WITTENBERG. L. M.

123.

Attributed to Martin Luther.

Before Jehovah's awful throne, Ye nations, bow with sacred joy,
Know that the Lord is God alone; He can create, and he destroy.

127. BOYCE. S. M.

From Dr. Boyce.

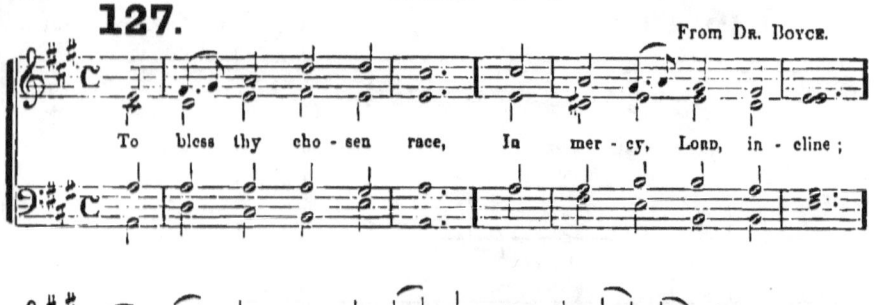

To bless thy cho-sen race, In mer-cy, Lord, in-cline;
And cause the brightness of thy face On all thy saints to shine.

128. CAMBRIDGE. S. M.

R. Harrison.

Come, ye that love the Lord, And let your joys be known
Join in a song of sweet ac-cord, And thus sur-round the throne.

129. CARLISLE. S. M. — Lockhart

My soul with patience waits For thee, the living Lord;
My hopes are on thy promise built, Thy never-failing word.

130. CHRIST'S CHURCH. S. M. — S. S. Wesley

To God, in whom I trust, I lift my heart and voice;
O let me not be put to shame, Nor let thy foes rejoice.

FAIRFIELD. S. M.

133.

R. HARRISON.

Welcome, sweet day of rest, That saw the Lord arise;
Welcome to this reviving breast And these rejoicing eyes.

GIBBONS. S. M.

134.

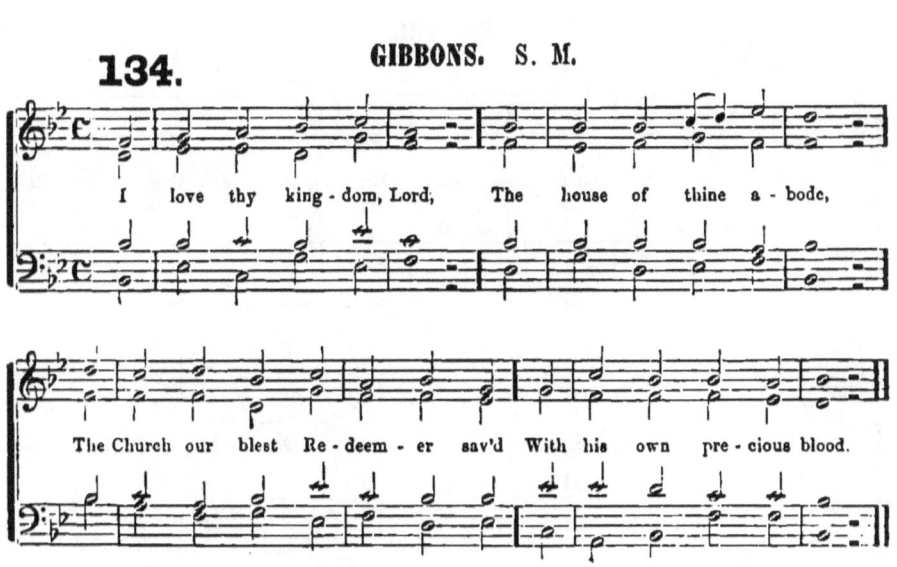

I love thy kingdom, Lord; The house of thine abode,
The Church our blest Redeemer sav'd With his own precious blood.

GORTON. S. M.

135. From BEETHOVEN.

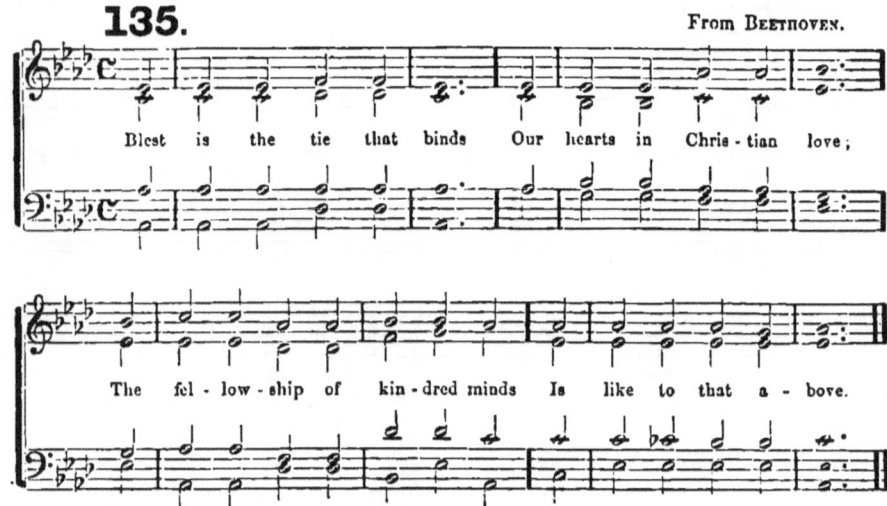

Blest is the tie that binds Our hearts in Christian love;
The fel-low-ship of kin-dred minds Is like to that a-bove.

HANDEL. S. M.

136. From HANDEL.

O bless the Lord, my soul, His grace to thee pro-claim;
And all that is with-in me, join To bless his ho-ly Name.

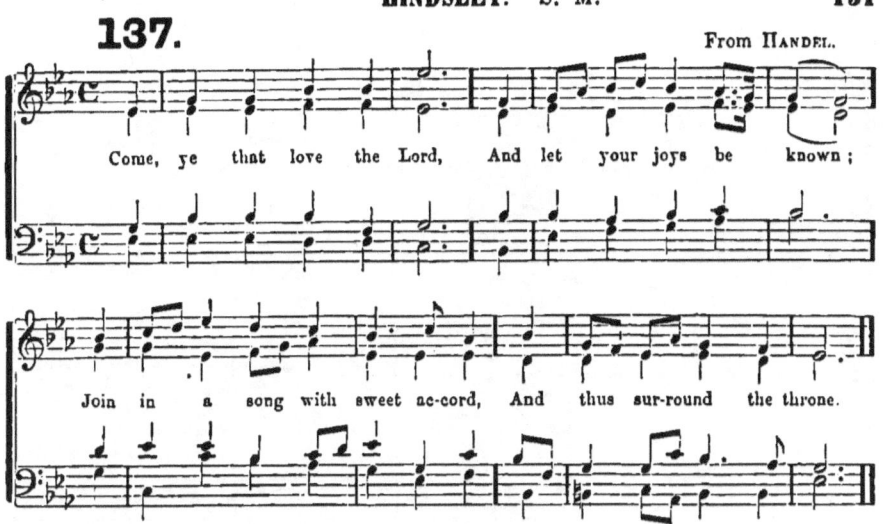

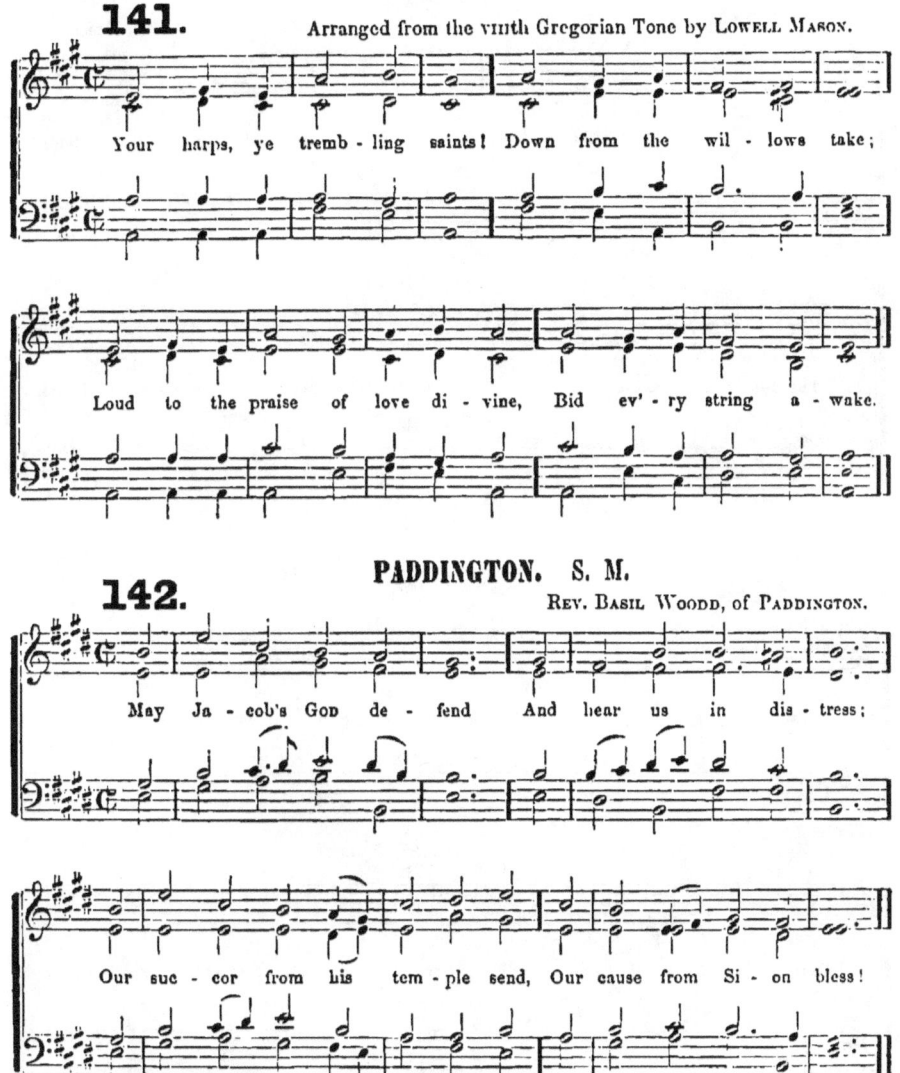

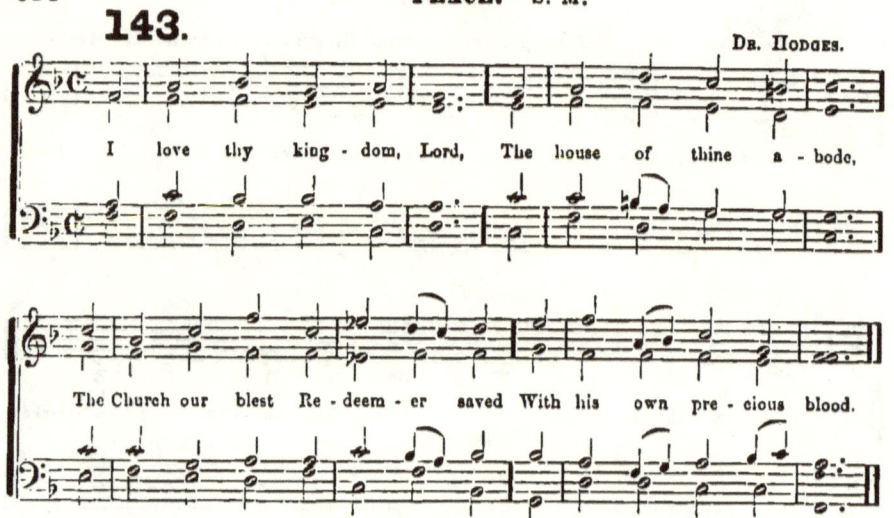

ST. BENEDICT. S. M.
147.

ST. BRIDE'S. S. M.
148. Dr. Howard.

ST. LAURENCE. S. M.

149.

De-fend me, Lord, from shame, For still I trust in thee;
As just and righteous is thy Name, From dan-ger set me free.

ST. MICHAEL'S. S. M.
From Day's Psalter, 1588.
In parts, by Rev. W. H. Havergal.

150.

O bless the Lord, my soul, His grace to thee pro-claim;
And all that is with-in me, join To bless his ho-ly Name.

ST. THOMAS. S. M.

151. A. WILLIAMS.

Heirs of unending life, While yet we sojourn here,
O let us our salvation work With trembling and with fear.

TYTHERTON, (or Croydon.) S. M.

152. REV. J. WEST, 1800.

The Spirit, in our hearts, Is whispering, sinner, Come;
The Bride, the Church of Christ, proclaims To all his children, Come.

2 Then, though our solitary coast,
The desert features soon were lost;
Thy temples there arose:
Our shores, as culture made them fair,
Were hallowed by thy rites, by prayer,
And blossomed as the rose.

3 And O, may we repay this debt
To regions solitary yet,
Within our spreading land:
There, brethren, from our common home,
Still westward, like our fathers, roam;
Still guided by thy hand.

4 Saviour, we own this debt of love:
O shed thy Spirit from above,
To move each Christian breast,
Till heralds shall thy truth proclaim,
And temples rise to fix thy Name,
Through all our desert west

GLORIA PATRI.
To FATHER, SON, and HOLY GHOST,
The God, whom heaven's triumphant host,
And saints on earth adore;
Be glory as in ages past,
As now it is, and so shall last
When time shall be no more.

GUILBERT. H. 1. or C. P. M. (8,8,6; 8,8,6.)

157. W. H. Walter. 1860.

1. With joy shall I be-hold the day That calls my wil-ling soul a-way, To dwell a-mong the blest: For lo! my great Re-deem-er's pow'r Un-folds the ev-er-last-ing door, And points me to his rest.

2 Ev'n now, to my expecting eyes,
   The heav'n-built towers of Salem rise;
     Their glory I survey;
   I view her mansions that contain
   The angel host, a beauteous train,
     And shine with cloudless day.

3 Thither, from earth's remotest end,
   Lo! the redeem'd of God ascend,
     Borne on immortal wing;
   There, crown'd with everlasting joy,
   In ceaseless hymns their tongues employ
     Before th'Almighty King.

4 The King a seat hath there prepared,
   High, on eternal base uprear'd,
     For his eternal Son:
   His palaces with joy abound;
   His saints, by him with glory crown'd,
     Attend and share his throne.

5 Mother of cities! o'er thy head
   Bright peace, with healing wings outspread,
     For evermore shall dwell:
   Let me, blest seat! my name behold
   Among thy citizens enroll'd,
     And bid the world farewell.

144

158.   HABAKKUK.   II. 1. or C. P. M. (8,8,6; 8,8,6.)

Dr. Hodges.

Although the vine its fruit deny, The budding fig-tree droop and die,

No oil the olive yield; Yet will I trust me in my God,

Yea, bend rejoicing to his rod, And by his grace be heal'd.

2 Though fields, in verdure once array'd,
By whirlwinds desolate be laid,
  Or parch'd by scorching beam;
Still in the Lord shall be my trust,
My joy; for, though his frown is just,
  His mercy is supreme.

3 Though from the fold the flock decay,
Though herds lie famish'd o'er the lea,
  And round the empty stall;
My soul above the wreck shall rise,
Its better joys are in the skies;
  There God is all in all.

4 In God my strength, howe'er distrest,
I yet will hope, and calmly rest,
  Nay, triumph in his love:
My lingering soul, my tardy feet,
Free as the hind he makes, and fleet,
  To speed my course above.

GLORIA PATRI.
To FATHER, SON, and HOLY GHOST,
To GOD whom heav'n's triumphant host,
  And saints on earth adore;
Be glory as in ages past,
As now it is, and so shall last
  When time shall be no more.

HARWOOD. H. 1, or C. P. M. (8, 8, 6; 8, 8, 6.) 145

159. HARWOOD.

1. Begin, my soul, th'exalted lay; Let each enraptur'd thought obey, And praise th'Almighty's Name; Let heaven and earth, and seas and skies, In one melodious concert rise, To swell th'inspiring theme.

2 Ye angels, catch the thrilling sound,
  While all th' adoring thrones around
    His boundless mercy sing;
  Let every listening saint above
  Wake all the tuneful soul of love,
    And touch the sweetest string.

3 Whate'er this living world contains,
  That wings the air, or treads the plains,
    United praise bestow;
  Ye tenants of the ocean wide,
  Proclaim Him through the mighty tide,
    And in the deeps below.

4 Let man, by nobler passions sway'd,
  The feeling heart, the judging head,
    In heavenly praise employ;
  Spread HIS tremendous name around
  While heaven's broad arch rings back the sound
    The general burst of joy.

GLORIA PATRI.

TO FATHER, SON, and HOLY GHOST,
The GOD whom heaven's triumphant host
  And saints on earth adore;
Be glory as in ages past,
As now it is, and so shall last
  When time shall be no more.

TREVES. II. 1. or C. P. M. (8,8,6; 8,8,6.)

160.

Heinrich Isaac. 1490.

1. Ye fields of light, ce-les-tial plains, Where pure, se-rene ef-ful-gence reigns,
Ye scenes di-vine-ly fair, Your Ma-ker's won-drous pow'r pro-claim;
Tell how he form'd your shin-ing frame, And breath'd the flu-id air.

2 Join all ye stars, the vocal choir;
Thou dazzling orb of liquid fire,
 The mighty chorus aid;
And, soon as evening veils the plain,
Thou moon, prolong the hallow'd strain,
 And praise Him in the shade.

3 Thou heaven of heavens, his vast abode,
Proclaim the glories of thy God;
 Ye worlds, declare his might;
He spake the word, and ye were made,
Darkness and dismal chaos fled,
 And nature sprung to light.

4 Let every element rejoice;
Ye thunders, burst with awful voice
 To Him who bids you roll;
His praise in softer notes declare,
Each whispering breeze of yielding air,
 And breathe it to the soul.

GLORIA PATRI.

To FATHER, SON, and HOLY GHOST,
The God, whom heaven's triumphant host,
 And saints on earth adore;
Be glory as in ages past,
As now it is, and so shall last
 When time shall be no more.

BERNE. II. 2, or L. P. M. (8, 8, 8; 8, 8, 8.) 147

161.

JOHANN SCHOP. 1660.

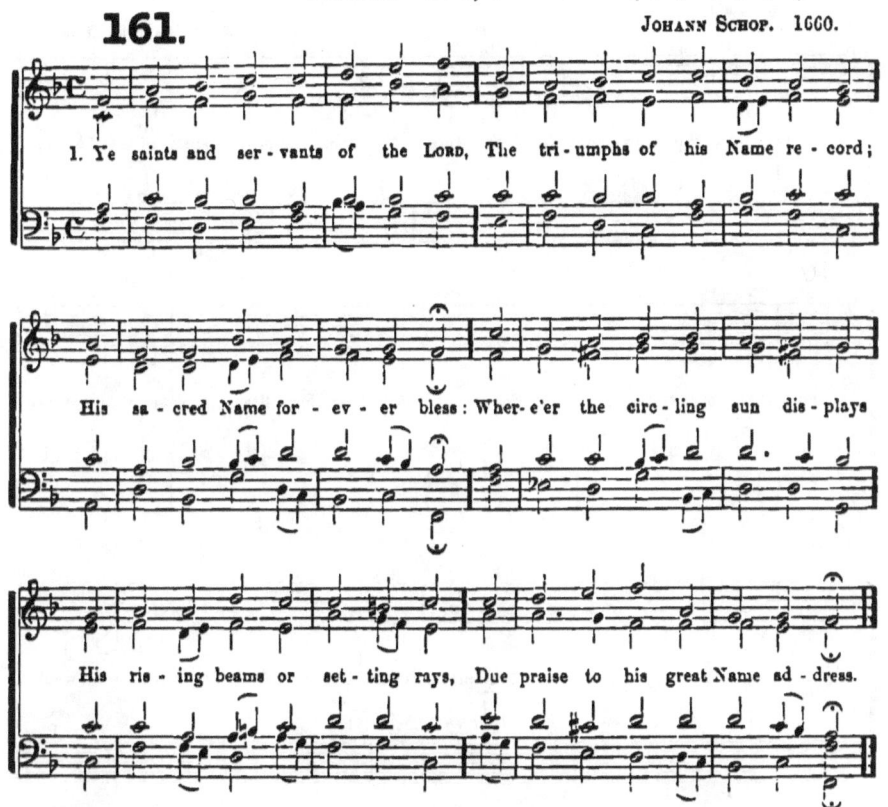

1. Ye saints and servants of the Lord, The triumphs of his Name record; His sacred Name for-ev-er bless: Wher-e'er the circ-ling sun dis-plays His ris-ing beams or set-ting rays, Due praise to his great Name ad-dress.

2. God through the world extends his sway;
The regions of eternal day
But shadows of his glory are;
With him whose majesty excels,
Who made the heaven in which he dwells
Let no created power compare.

3. Though 'tis beneath his state to view
In highest heaven what angels do;
Yet he to earth vouchsafes his care:
He takes the needy from his cell,
Advancing him in courts to dwell,
Companion of the greatest there

GLORIA PATRI.

To FATHER, SON, and HOLY GHOST,
The GOD whom heaven's triumphant host
And suff'ring saints on earth adore;
Be glory as in ages past,
As now it is and so shall last
When time itself shall be no more.

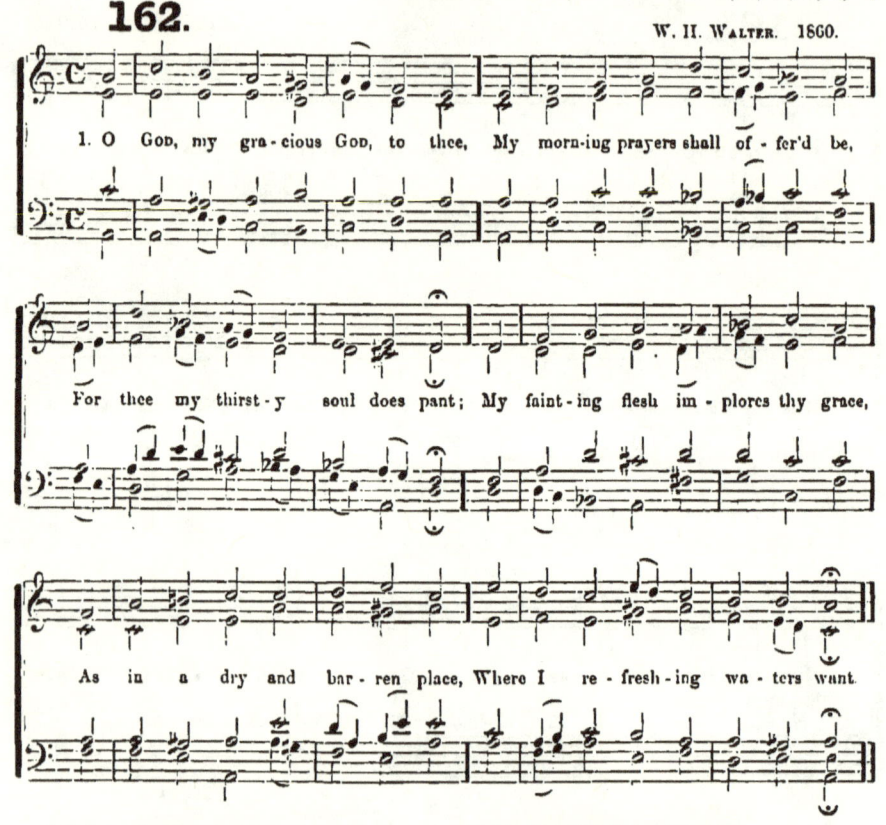

2 O, to my longing eyes once more
That view of glorious power restore,
Which thy majestic house displays;
Because to me thy wondrous love
Than life itself does dearer prove,
My lips shall always speak thy praise.

3 My life, while I that life enjoy,
In blessing God I will employ,
With lifted hands adore his Name:
As with its choicest food supplied,
My soul shall be full satisfied,
While I with joy his praise proclaim

4 When down I lie, sweet sleep to find,
Thou, Lord, art present to my mind.
And when I wake in dead of night;
Because thou still dost succor bring,
Beneath the shadow of thy wing
I rest with safety and delight.

MELCHISEDEC. H. 2. or L. P. M. (8, 8, 8; 8, 8, 8.)

163. W. H. WALTER. 1854.

1. The Lord un-to my Lord thus spake: "Till I thy foes thy foot-stool make, Sit thou in state at my right hand; Su-preme in Si-on thou shalt be, And all thy proud op-pos-ers see Sub-ject-ed to thy just com-mand."

2 "Thee, in thy power's triumphant day,
　The willing people shall obey ;
　And, when thy rising beams they view,
Shall all, (redeem'd from error's night,)
　Appear more numerous and bright
　Than crystal drops of morning dew."

3 The Lord hath sworn, nor sworn in vain,
　That, like Melchisedec's, thy reign
　And priesthood shall no period see :
Anointed Prince ! thou, bending low,
　Shalt drink where darkest torrents flow
　Then raise thy head in victory !

GLORIA PATRI.

To FATHER, SON. and HOLY GHOST,
　The GOD whom heaven's triumphant host
　And suff'ring saints on earth adore ;
Be glory as in ages past,
　As now it is, and so shall last
　When time itself shall be no more.

NEWCOURT. H. 2. or L. P. M. (8, 8, 8; 8, 8, 8.)
H. Bond.

1. God is our refuge in distress, A present help when dangers press, In him, undaunted we'll confide; Though earth were from her centre tost, And mountains in the ocean lost, Torn piece-meal by the roaring tide.

2 A gentler stream with gladness still
  The city of our Lord shall fill,
   The royal seat of God most high:
  God dwells in Sion, whose fair towers
  Shall mock th' assaults of earthly powers,
   While his almighty aid is nigh.

3 Submit to God's almighty sway,
  For him the heathen shall obey,
   And earth her Sovereign Lord confess:
  The God of hosts conducts our arms,
  Our tower of refuge in alarms,
   As to our fathers in distress.

Gloria Patri.
To Father, Son, and Holy Ghost,
The God whom heaven's triumphant host
 And suff'ring saints on earth adore;
Be glory as in ages past,
As now it is, and so shall last
 When time itself shall be no more.

RAVENSCROFT. H. 2. or L. P. M. (8,8,8; 8,8,8.) 151

165.
Thos. Ravenscroft.

1. The Lord hath spoke, the mighty God Hath sent his summons all abroad, From dawning light till day declines; The listening earth his voice hath heard, And he from Sion hath appear'd, Where beauty in perfection shines.

2 Our God shall come, and keep no more
  Misconstrued silence as before,
  But wasting flames before him send ;
  Around shall tempests fiercely rage,
  While he does heaven and earth engage
  His just tribunal to attend.

3 Assemble all my saints to me,
  (Thus runs the great divine decree)
  That in my lasting covenant live,
  And offerings bring with constant care ;
  The heavens his justice shall declare,
  For God himself shall sentence give.

Gloria Patri.
To Father, Son, and Holy Ghost,
The God whom heaven's triumphant host,
  And suffering saints on earth adore ;
Be glory as in ages past,
As now it is, and so shall last
  When time itself shall be no more.

154

EATON. H. 3, or L. M. 6 lines.

169.

God's temple crowns the ho-ly mount, The Lord there con - de-scends to dwell;

His Si-on's gates, in his ac - count, Our Is-rael's fair-est tents ex-cel:

Yea, glo-rious things of thee we sing, O ci - ty of th'Almighty King!

GRISWOLD. 11. 3. or L. M. 6 lines.

170.

Arranged from Mozart.

Peace, troubled soul, whose plain-tive moan Hath taught each scene the note of woe;

156

172. SALISBURY, (New.) H. 3. or L. M. 6 lines.
Arranged from HAYDN.

Great God, this sa - cred day of thine De-mands the soul's col - lect - ed powers;

Glad - ly we now to thee re - sign These so - lemn, con - se - cra - ted hours:

O may our souls a - dor - ing own The grace that calls us to thy throne.

173. ST. STEPHEN. H. 3, or L. M. 6 lines.
GEORGE NEUMARK. 1650.

As, pant - ing in the sul - try beam, The hart de - sires the cool - ing stream,

ST. STEPHEN. (Concluded.) 157

So to thy pre-sence, Lord, I flee, So longs my soul, O God, for thee;

A-thirst to taste thy liv-ing grace, And see thy glo-ry, face to face.

174. BETHESDA. II. 4. or H. M.

Dr. Greene.

Lord of the worlds a-bove! How pleasant and how fair, The dwellings of thy love, Thine earthly tem-ples are! To thine a-bode my heart as-pires With warm de-sires to see my God.

IRENÆUS. H. 4. or H. M. 159

177.
Rev. W. H. Havergal.

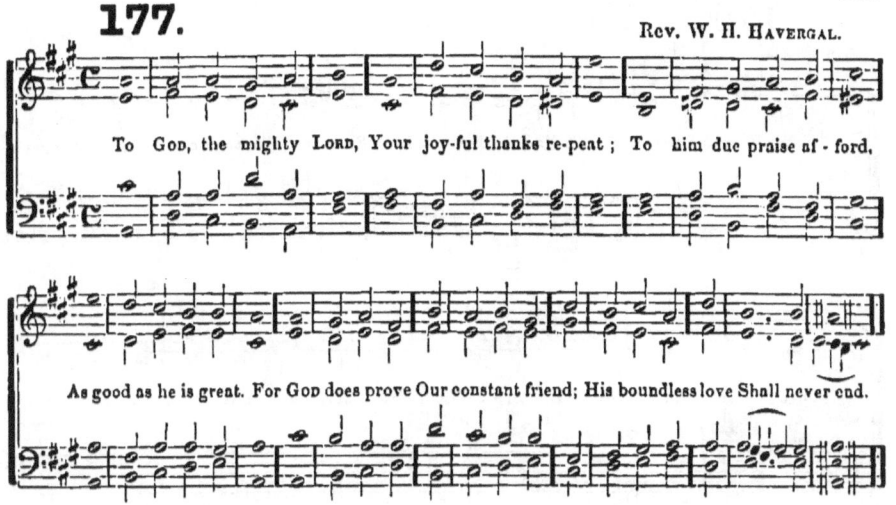

To God, the mighty Lord, Your joyful thanks repeat; To him due praise afford,
As good as he is great. For God does prove Our constant friend; His boundless love Shall never end.

LEIPSIC. H. 4. or H. M.

178.
Johann Cruger. 1662.

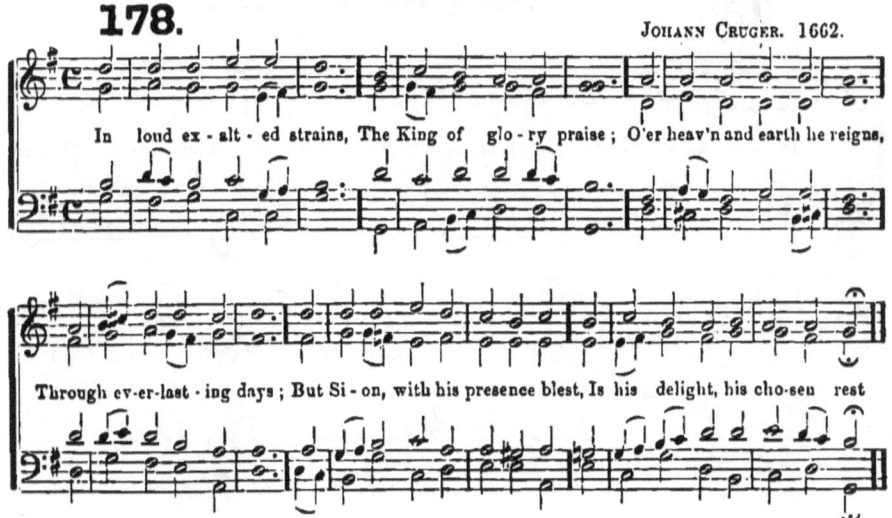

In loud exalted strains, The King of glory praise; O'er heav'n and earth he reigns,
Through everlasting days; But Sion, with his presence blest, Is his delight, his chosen rest.

ST. JOHN'S. H. 4, or H. M.

181. From the "Parish Choir."

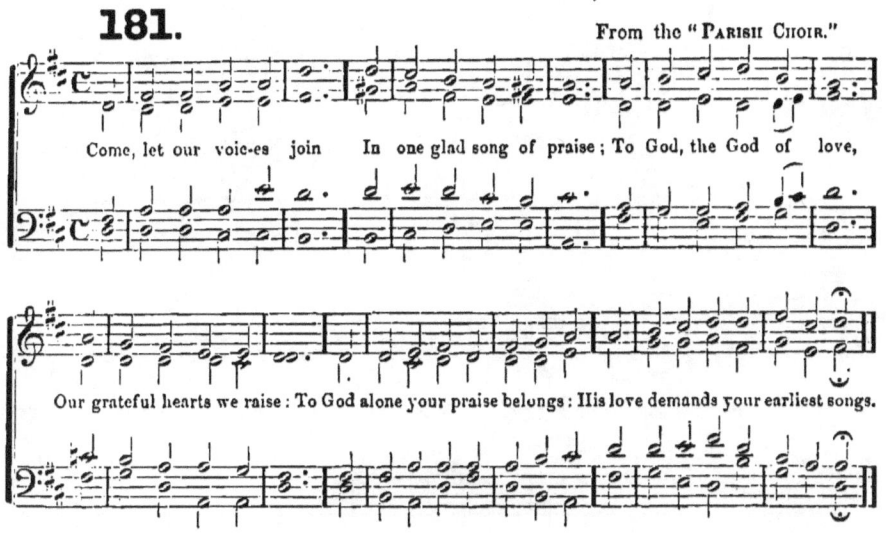

Come, let our voic-es join In one glad song of praise; To God, the God of love, Our grateful hearts we raise: To God alone your praise belongs: His love demands your earliest songs.

ST. PHILIP'S. H. 4, or H. M.

182. LEVESQUE.

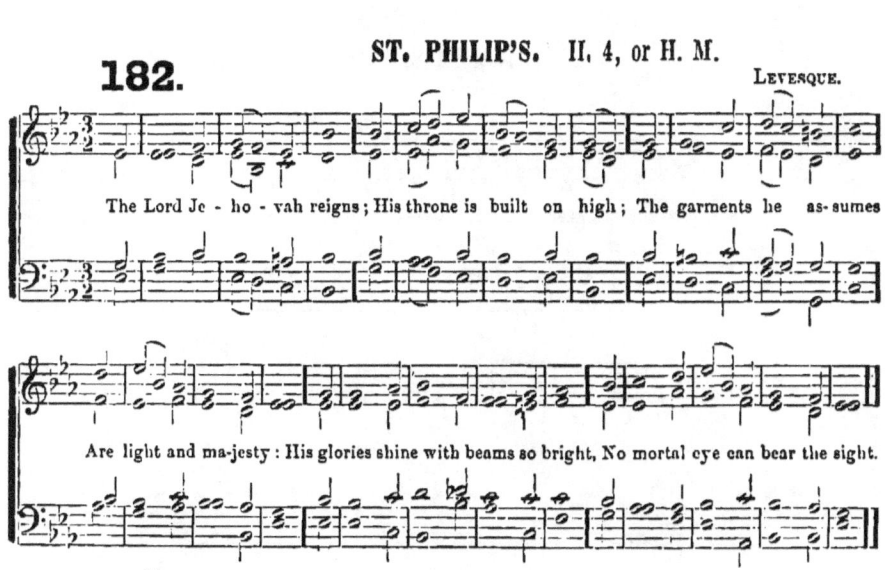

The Lord Je-ho-vah reigns; His throne is built on high; The garments he as-sumes Are light and ma-jesty: His glories shine with beams so bright, No mortal eye can bear the sight.

TRIUMPH. H. 4, or H. M.

183. Lockhart.

Re-joice! the Lord is King! Your God and King a-dore; Mortals! give thanks, and sing, And tri-umph ev-ermore: Lift up your heart, lift up your voice! Rejoice, aloud, ye saints, rejoice.

WARSAW. H. 4, or H. M.

184. T. Clark.

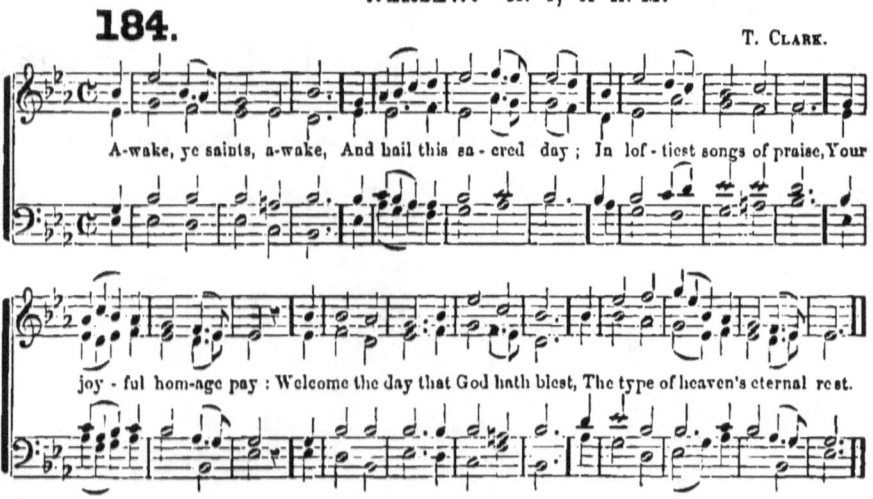

A-wake, ye saints, a-wake, And hail this sa-cred day; In lof-tiest songs of praise, Your joy-ful hom-age pay: Welcome the day that God hath blest, The type of heaven's eternal rest.

CALCOTT. 11. 5, or 10s. 163

185.

Dr. Calcott.

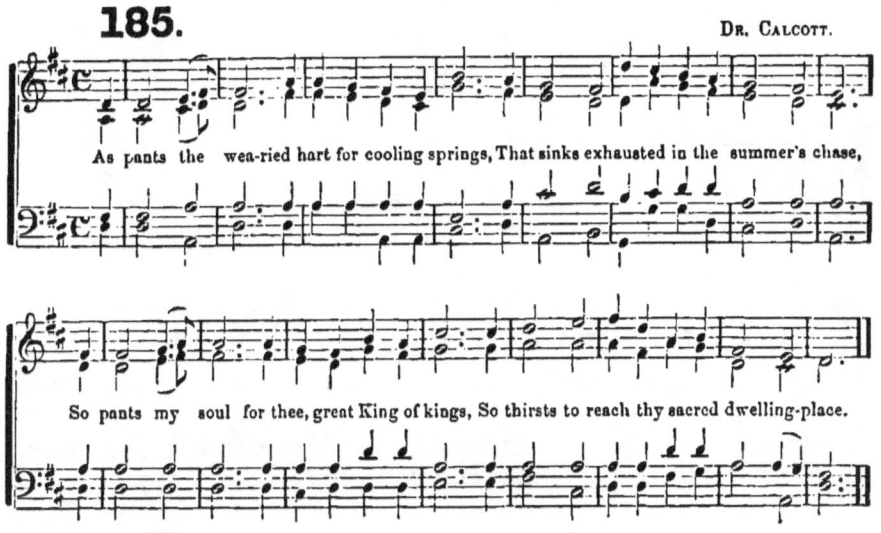

As pants the wea-ried hart for cooling springs, That sinks exhausted in the summer's chase,

So pants my soul for thee, great King of kings, So thirsts to reach thy sacred dwelling-place.

REFUGE. 11. 5. or 10s.

186.

Gibbons.

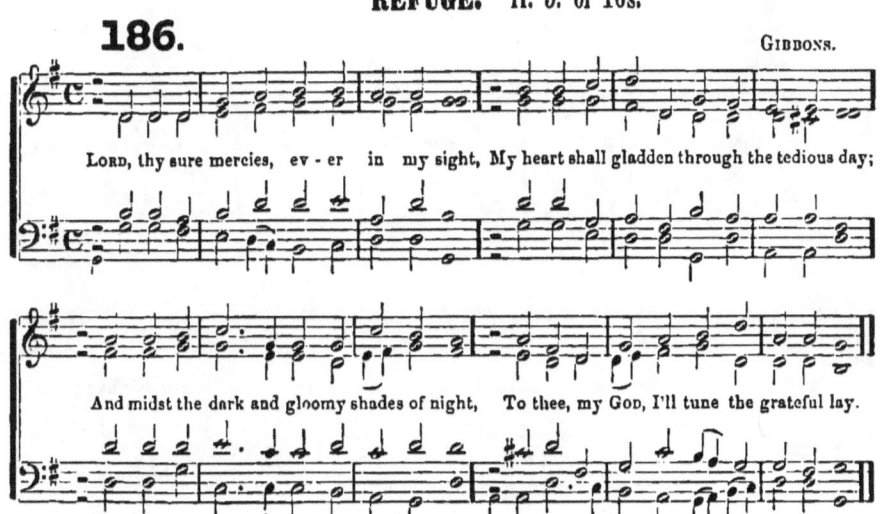

Lord, thy sure mercies, ev-er in my sight, My heart shall gladden through the tedious day;

And midst the dark and gloomy shades of night, To thee, my God, I'll tune the grateful lay.

RUSSIAN HYMN. 11. 5. or 10s.

187. A. Lovoff.

Rise, crown'd with light, im-pe-rial Sa-lem rise; Ex-alt thy towering head and lift thine eyes: See heaven its sparkling portals wide dis-play, And break up-on thee in a flood of day.

ST. CLEMENT'S. 11. 5. or 10s.

188. W. H. Walter, 1856.

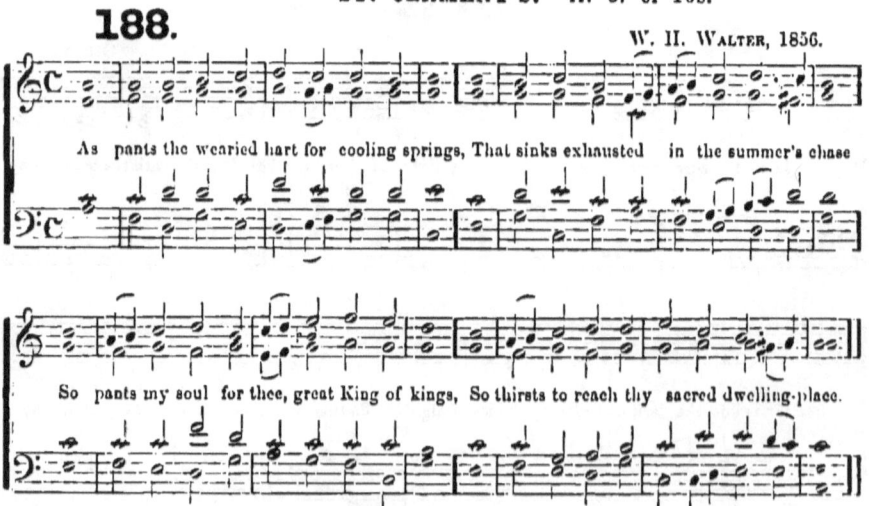

As pants the wearied hart for cooling springs, That sinks exhausted in the summer's chase So pants my soul for thee, great King of kings, So thirsts to reach thy sacred dwelling-place.

EPIPHANY. H. G, or 7s and 6s. 165

189.

W. H. WALTER. 1852.

Hail to the Lord's Anointed, Great David's greater Son;

Hail in the time appointed, His reign on earth begun!

He comes to break oppression, To set the captive free;

To take away transgression, And rule in equity.

170

194. ANGELUS. III. 1. or 7s.

Sov'-reign Ru-ler of the skies, Ev-er gra-cious, ev-er wise,
All our times are in thy hand, All e-vents at thy com-mand.

195. BLOOMFIELD. III. 1. or 7s.

Sin-ner, rouse thee from thy sleep, Wake, and o'er thy fol-ly weep:
Raise thy spir-it, dark and dead, Je-sus waits his light to shed.

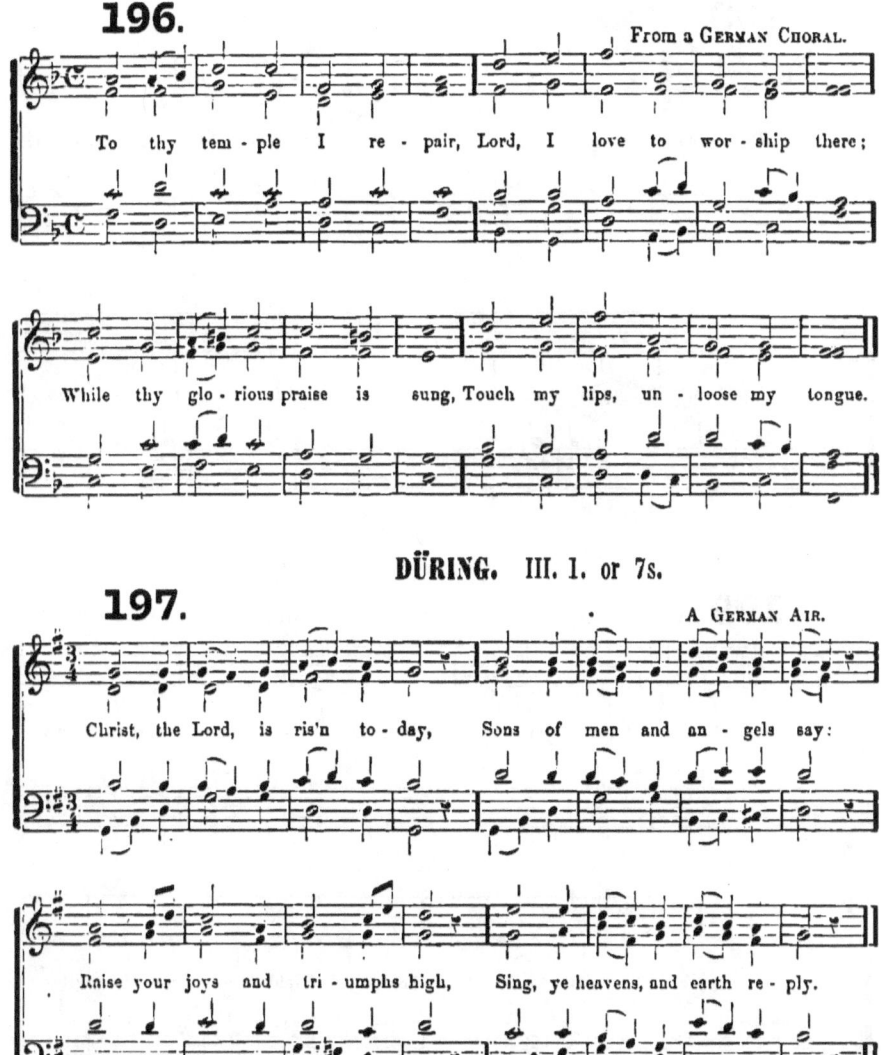

EDYFIELD. III. 1. or 7s.

198.

Hast-en, sin-ner, to be wise; Stay not for the mor-row's sun:
Wis-dom, if you still de-spise, Hard-er is it to be won.

EVEN-SONG. III. 1. or 7s.

199.

Melody from the "Parish Choir."

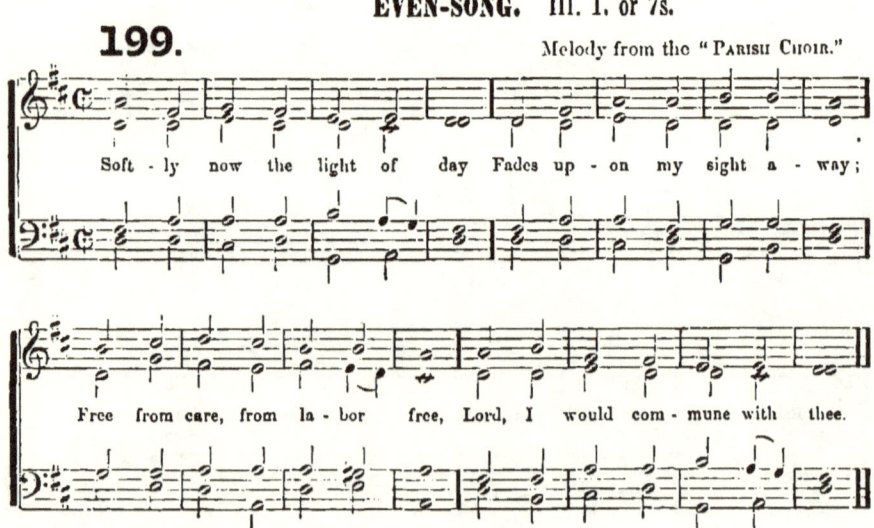

Soft-ly now the light of day Fades up-on my sight a-way;
Free from care, from la-bor free, Lord, I would com-mune with thee.

INNOCENTS. III. 1, or 7s.

200.

From the "Parish Choir."

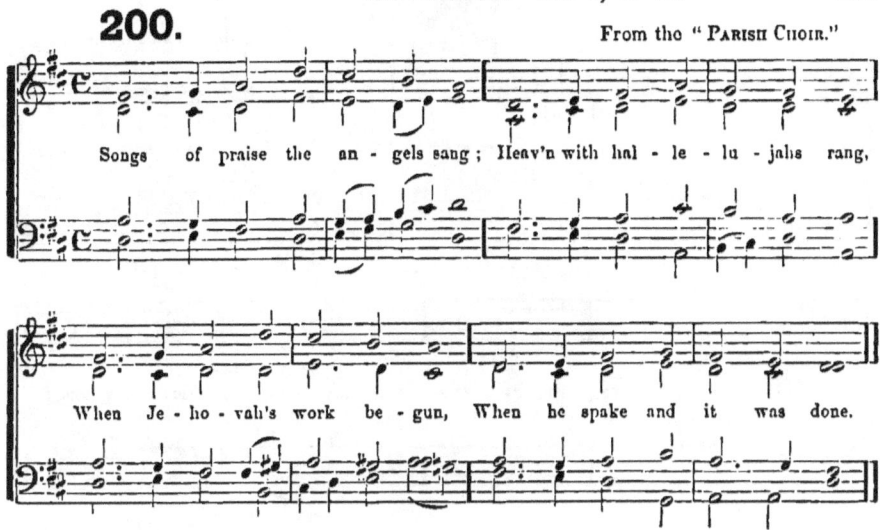

GLORIA PATRI. III. 1, or 7s.

201.

MAGDALEN. III. 1, or 7s.

From the "PARISH CHOIR."

To thy temple I repair, Lord, I love to worship there;
While thy glorious praise is sung, Touch my lips, un-loose my tongue.

NUREMBERG. III 1, or 7s.

From a GERMAN CHORAL.

Magnify Jehovah's Name; For his mercies ever sure;
From eternity the same, To eternity endure.

PLEYEL'S HYMN. III. 1, or 7s. 175

204. PLEYEL.

Chil-dren of the heav'n-ly King, As we jour-ney, let us sing; Sing the Sa-viour's wor-thy praise, Glo-rious in his works and ways.

SHARON. III. 1, or 7s.✱

205.

Lord, for ev-er at thy side, Let my place and por-tion be; Strip me of the robe of pride, Clothe me with hu-mil-i-ty.

✱ Or III. 3, 8s & 7s, by omitting the slurs at the end of the 1st and 3d lines.

ST. AIDEN'S. III. 1, or 7s.

Hast-en, sin-ner, to be wise; Stay not for the mor-row's sun; Wis-dom, if you still de-spise, Hard-er is it to be won.

ST. AMBROSE. III. 1, or 7s.

Sin-ner, rouse thee from thy sleep, Wake, and o'er thy fol-ly weep; Raise thy spir-it dark and dead, Je-sus waits his light to shed.

THEODORA. III. 1. or 7s.

208. Arranged from HANDEL.

Sing, my soul, His wond-rous love, Who, from yon bright throne a-bove,

Ev-er watch-ful o'er our race, Still to man ex-tends his grace.

WEBER. III. 1. or 7s.

209. From VON WEBER.

Soft-ly now the light of day Fades up-on my sight a-way;

Free from care, from la-bour free, Lord, I would com-mune with thee.

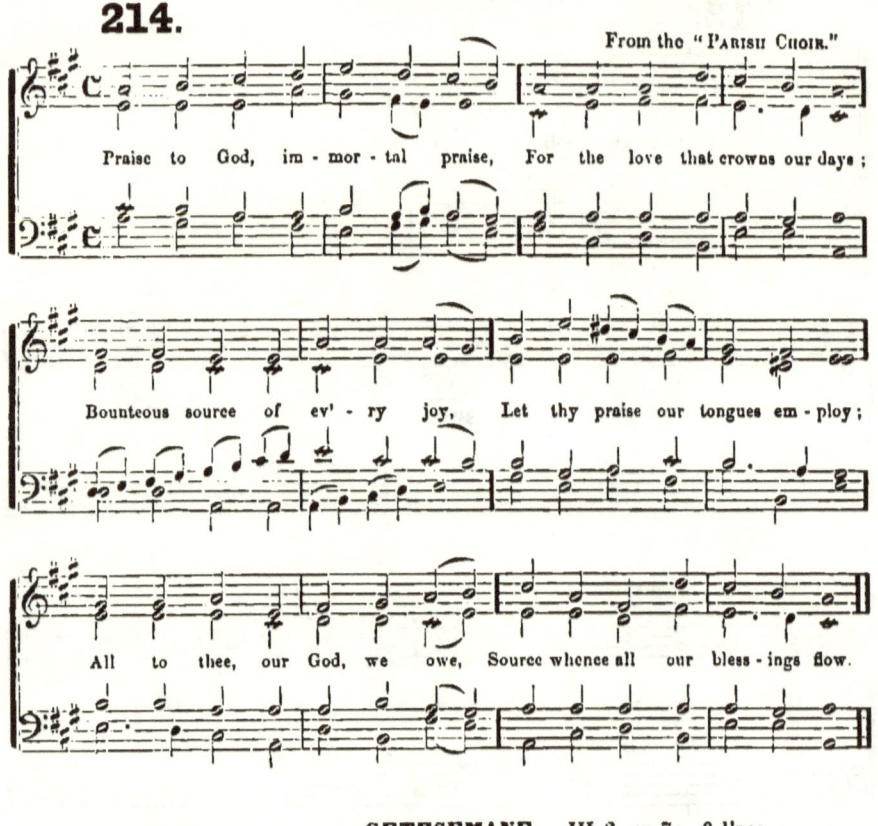

GETHSEMANE. (Concluded.) 183

Your Redeemer's conflict see; Watch with Him one bitter hour;
Turn not from His grief away, Learn of Jesus Christ to pray.

GRATITUDE. III. 2, or 7s, 6 lines.

216.

A German Choral.

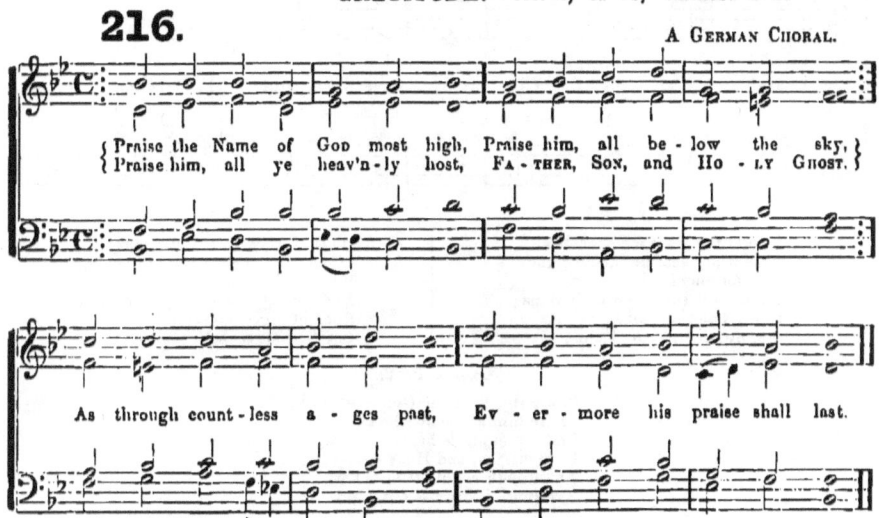

{ Praise the Name of God most high, Praise him, all below the sky, }
{ Praise him, all ye heav'n-ly host, Father, Son, and Holy Ghost. }
As through countless ages past, Evermore his praise shall last.

"ROCK OF AGES." III. 2, or 7s, 6 lines.

217.

Choral harmonized by W. T. Best.

1. Rock of Ages, cleft for me, Let me hide myself in thee;
Let the water and the blood, From thy side a healing flood,
Be of sin the double cure, Save from wrath, and make me pure.

2 Should my tears for ever flow,
Should my zeal no languor know,
This for sin could not atone,
Thou must save, and thou alone;
In my hand no price I bring,
Simply to thy cross I cling.

3 While I draw this fleeting breath,
When mine eyelids close in death,
When I rise to worlds unknown,
And behold thee on thy throne,
Rock of Ages, cleft for me,
Let me hide myself in thee

GLORIA PATRI.

Praise the Name of God most high,
Praise him all below the sky,
Praise him all ye heavenly host,
FATHER, SON, and HOLY GHOST;
As through countless ages past,
Evermore his praise shall last.

ANFIELD. III. 3, or 8s & 7s.   185

218.   WRANISKY.

Sa-viour, source of ev'-ry bless-ing, Tune my heart to grate-ful lays;
Streams of mer-cy, nev-er ceas-ing, Call for cease-less songs of praise.

219.   **CANTERBURY.** III. 3,* or 8s & 7s.

Hail! thou long-ex-pect-ed Je-sus, Born to set thy peo-ple free:
From our sins and fears re-lease us, Let us find our rest in thee.

* Or III. 5. (8s, 7s and 4s) by repeating the *first* half of the tune.

CHEETHAM. III. 3, or 8s & 7s.

W. H. Walter. 1850.

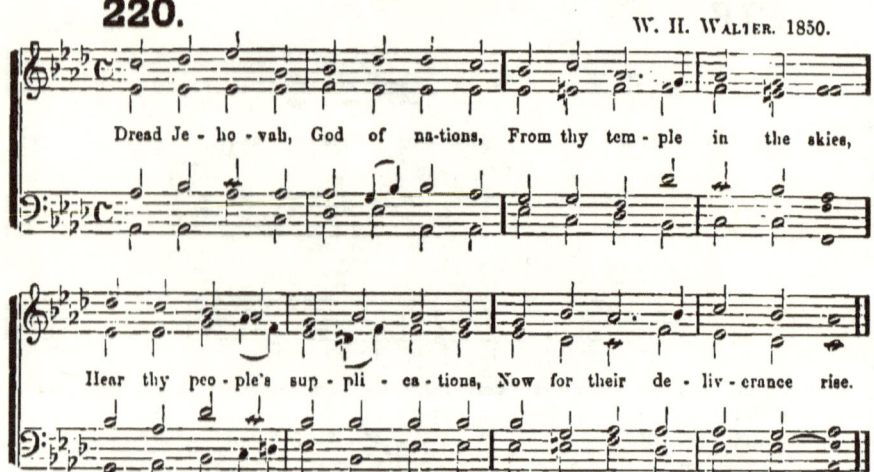

Dread Jehovah, God of nations, From thy temple in the skies,
Hear thy people's supplications, Now for their deliverance rise.

FRANKFORT. III. 3, or 8s & 7s.

Winter.

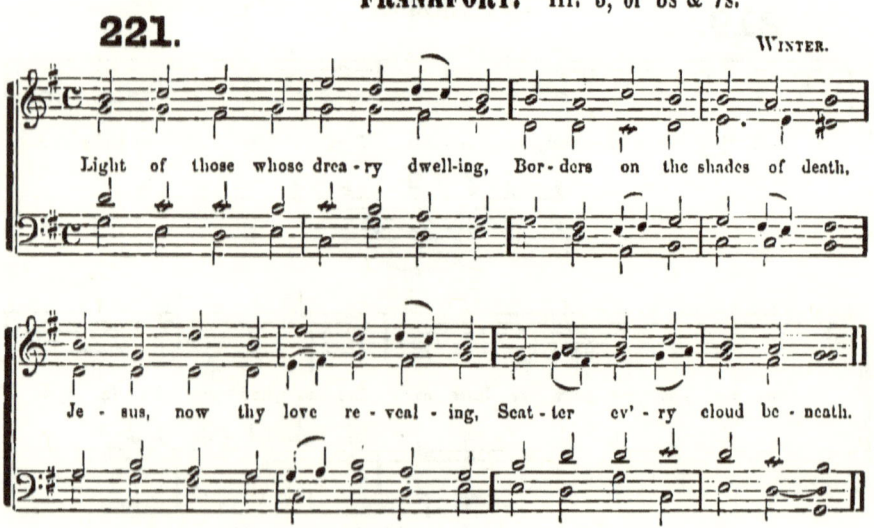

Light of those whose dreary dwelling, Borders on the shades of death,
Jesus, now thy love revealing, Scatter ev'ry cloud beneath.

HAVERGAL. III. 3, or 8s & 7s.

222. Rev. WM. H. HAVERGAL.

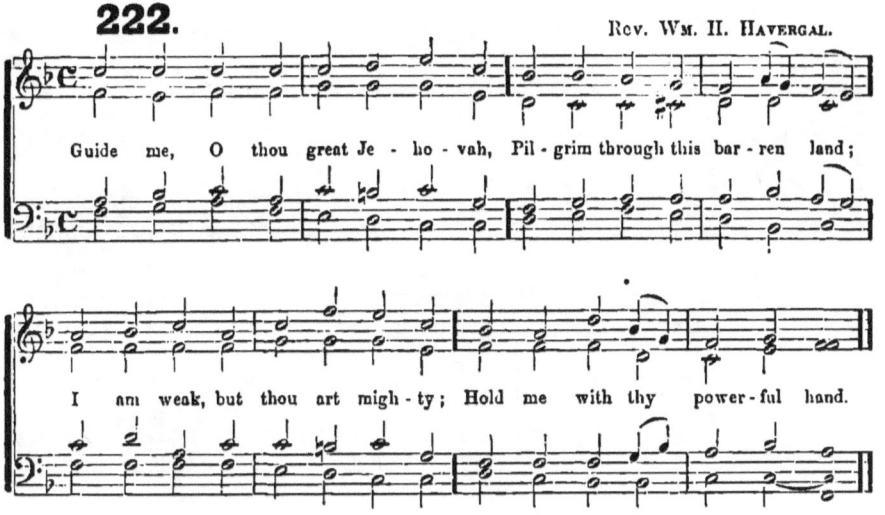

Guide me, O thou great Je-ho-vah, Pil-grim through this bar-ren land;
I am weak, but thou art migh-ty; Hold me with thy pow-er-ful hand.

MANHEIM. III. 3, or 8s & 7s.

223. From BEETHOVEN.

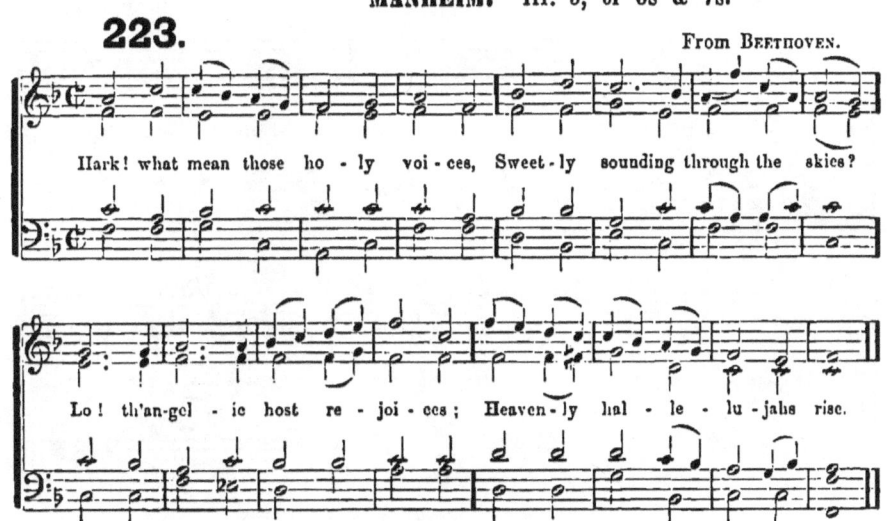

Hark! what mean those ho-ly voi-ces, Sweet-ly sounding through the skies?
Lo! th'an-gel-ic host re-joi-ces; Heaven-ly hal-le-lu-jahs rise.

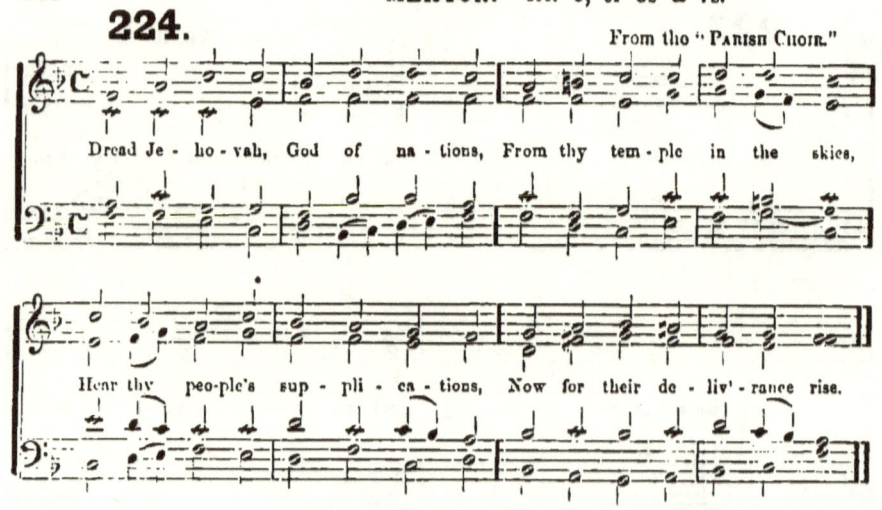

* Or III. 5, (8s, 7s & 4s,) by repeating the *last* half of the tune.

WALTHAM. III. 3, or 8s & 7s.

228.

Heinrich Albert, 1604.

Dread Jehovah, God of nations, From thy temple in the skies,
Hear thy people's supplications, Now for their deliv'rance rise.

WORTHING. III. 3, or 8s & 7s.

229.

Schelz.

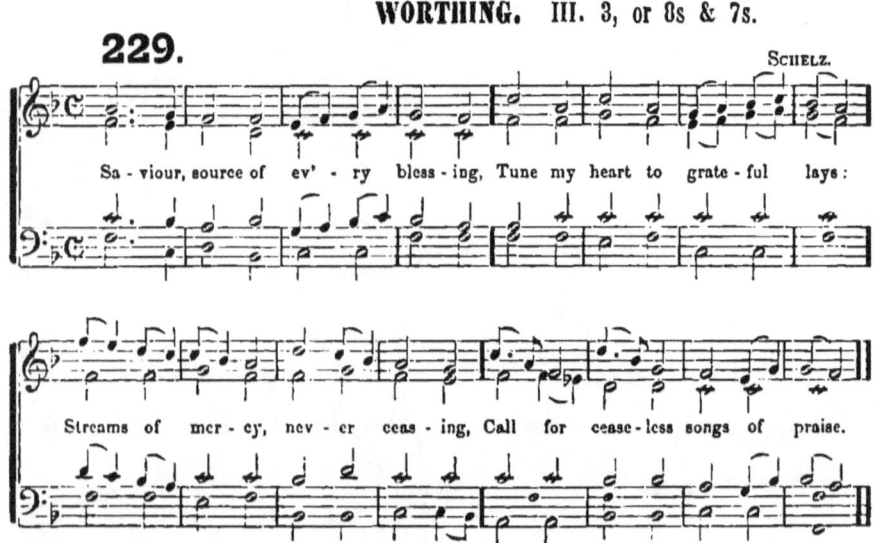

Saviour, source of ev'ry blessing, Tune my heart to grateful lays:
Streams of mercy, never ceasing, Call for ceaseless songs of praise.

ADORATION. III. 3, or 8s & 7s Double.

2 'Tis the Saviour, now victorious,
  Travelling onward in his might;
'Tis the Saviour, O how glorious
  To his people is the sight!
Satan conquered, and the grave,
Jesus now is strong to save.

3 Why that blood his raiment staining?
  'Tis the blood of many slain;
Of his foes there's none remaining,
  None, the contest to maintain:
Fall'n they are, no more to rise,
All their glory prostrate lies.

4 Mighty Victor, reign for ever,
  Wear the crown so dearly won!
Never shall thy people, never,
  Cease to sing what thou hast done!
Thou hast fought thy people's foes;
Thou hast heal'd thy people's woes!

GLORIA PATRI.
To the FATHER, throned in heaven,
  To the SAVIOUR, CHRIST, his SON,
To the SPIRIT, praise be given,
  Everlasting Three in One:
As of old, the Trinity
Still is worshipp'd, still shall be.

* Or III. 5, (8s, 7s and 4s,) by omitting the slur at the end of the 5th line.

VISION. III. 4.

234. W. H. Walter. 1860.

1. Who is this that comes from E-dom, All his raiment stain'd with blood, To the captive speaking freedom, Bringing and bestowing good; Glorious in the garb he wears, Glorious in the spoil he bears?

2 'Tis the Saviour, now victorious,
  Travelling onward in his might;
 'Tis the Saviour, O how glorious
  To his people is the sight!
 Satan conquered, and the grave,
 Jesus now is strong to save.

3 Why that blood his raiment staining?
  'Tis the blood of many slain;
 Of his foes there's none remaining
  None, the contest to maintain:
 Fall'n they are, no more to rise,
 All their glory prostrate lies.

4 Mighty Victor, reign for ever,
  Wear the crown so dearly won!
 Never shall thy people, never,
  Cease to sing what thou hast done!
 Thou hast fought thy people's foes;
 Thou hast heal'd thy people's woes!

GLORIA PATRI.
To the FATHER, throned in heaven,
 To the SAVIOUR, CHRIST, his SON,
To the SPIRIT, praise be given,
 Everlasting Three in One:
As of old, the Trinity
Still is worshipp'd, still shall be.

196

235. ADVENT HYMN. III. 5, or 8s, 7s, & 4s.

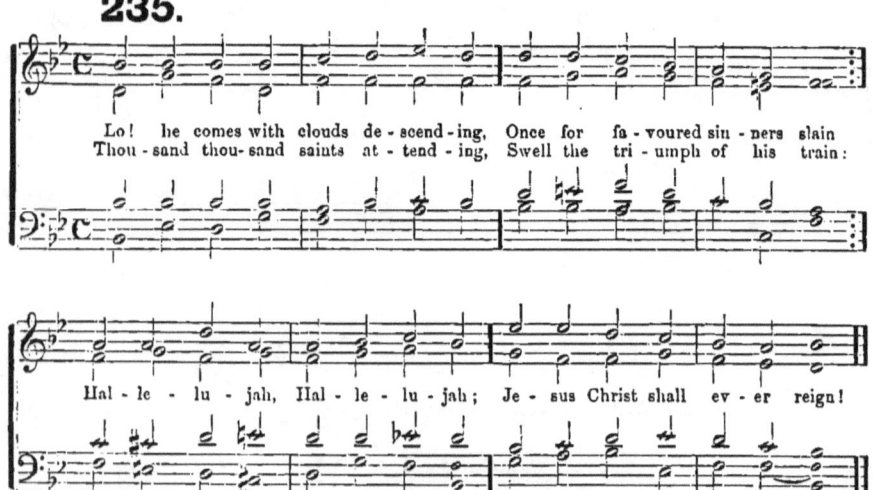

Lo! he comes with clouds de-scend-ing, Once for fa-voured sin-ners slain
Thou-sand thou-sand saints at-tend-ing, Swell the tri-umph of his train:
Hal-le-lu-jah, Hal-le-lu-jah; Je-sus Christ shall ev-er reign!

236. ERPINGHAM. III. 5, or 8s, 7s & 4s.

Lord, dis-miss us with thy bless-ing, Fill our hearts with joy and peace
Let us each thy love pos-sess-ing, Tri-umph in.. re-deem-ing grace:

ERPINGHAM. (Concluded.) 197

O re-fresh us, O re-fresh us, Trav'-ling through this wil-der-ness.

HAYDN'S HYMN. III. 5, or 8s, 7s & 4s.

237.

From J. HAYDN.

An-gels from the realms of glo-ry, Wing your flight o'er all the earth,

Ye who sang cre-a-tion's sto-ry, Now pro-claim Mes-si-ah's birth;

Come and wor-ship, Come and wor-ship, Wor-ship Christ, the new-born King.

238. JOANNA. 11I. 5, or 8s, 7s & 4s.
Theo. H. Smith.

Zi - on stands with hills sur - round - ed, Zi - on, kept by power di - vine:
All her foes shall be con - found - ed, Though the world in arms com - bine:
Hap - py Zi - on, Hap - py Zi - on, What a fa - vor'd lot is thine!

239. NOVELLO. III. 5, or 8s, 7s & 4s.
Vincent Novello.

On the mountain's top ap - pear - ing, Lo! the sa - cred her - ald stands
Wel - come news to Zi - on bear - ing, Zi - on, long in hos - tile lands.

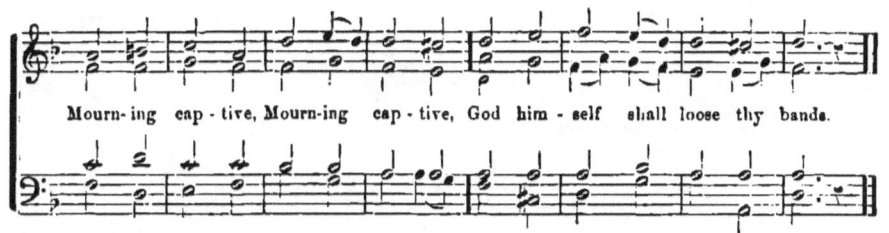

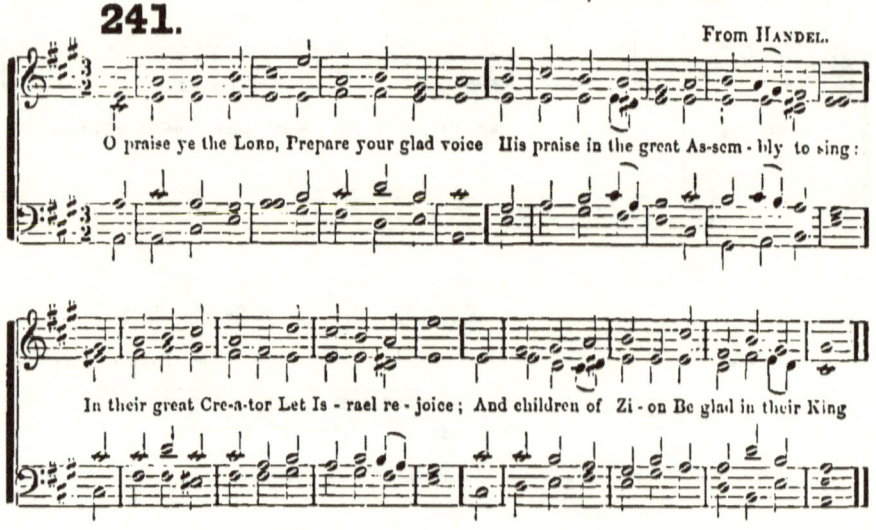

243. DEVOTION. IV. 2, or 8s.

244. GOSHEN. IV. 2, or 8s.

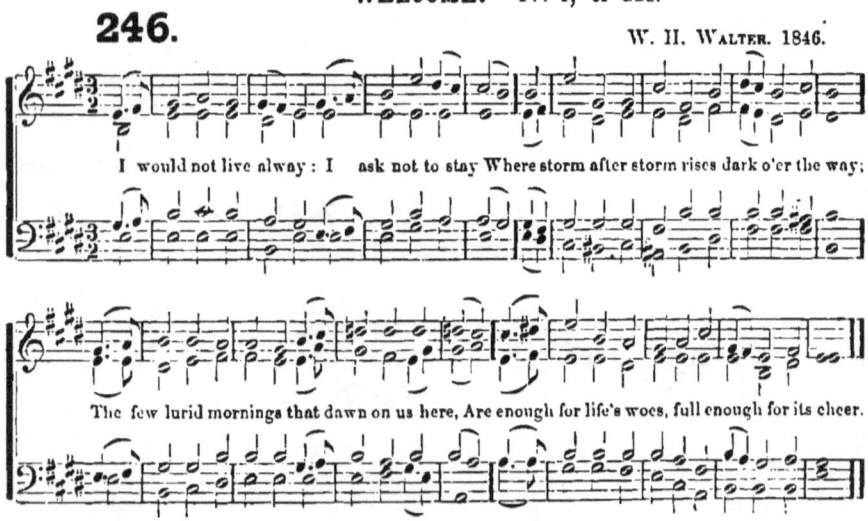

"ADESTE FIDELES." IV. 4,* or 11s.

247.

PORTUGUESE HYMN.

Come hith-er! ye faith-ful, Tri-umph-ant-ly sing! Come, see in the man-ger The an-gels' dread King! To Beth-le-hem hast-en, With joy-ful ac-cord.... Oh, come ye, come hith-er, Oh, come ye, come hith-er, Oh, come ye, come hith-er To wor-ship the Lord!

2 True Son of the Father,
   He comes from the skies ;
The womb of the virgin
   He doth not despise,
To Bethlehem hasten,
   With joyful accord,
Oh, come ye, come hither,
   To worship the Lord!

3 Hark! hark to the angels
   All singing in heaven,
"To God in the highest
   All glory be given!"
To Bethlehem hasten,
   With joyful accord,
Oh, come ye, come hither,
   To worship the Lord!

4 To Thee, then, O Jesus,
   This day of Thy birth,
Be glory and honour
   Through heaven and earth,
True Godhead Incarnate!
   Omnipotent Word!
Oh, come! let us hasten
   To worship the Lord!

5 Come, let us adore him,
   Come, bow at his feet,
O give him the glory,
   The praise that is meet ;
Let joyful hosannas
   Unceasing arise,
And join the full chorus
   That gladdens the skies.

* This tune will also suit the Hymn. "How firm a foundation, ye saints of the Lord."

AMSTERDAM. 7s & 6s. (Peculiar.) 205

250.

Dr. NARES.

1 { Rise, my soul, and stretch thy wings, Thy bet-ter por-tion trace;
    Rise from trans-i-to-ry things, Towards heav'n, thy des-tined place:

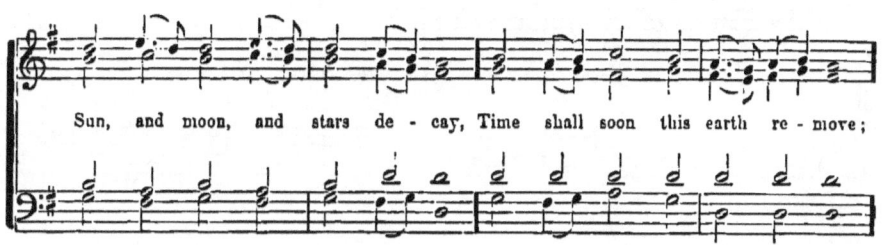

Sun, and moon, and stars de-cay, Time shall soon this earth re-move;

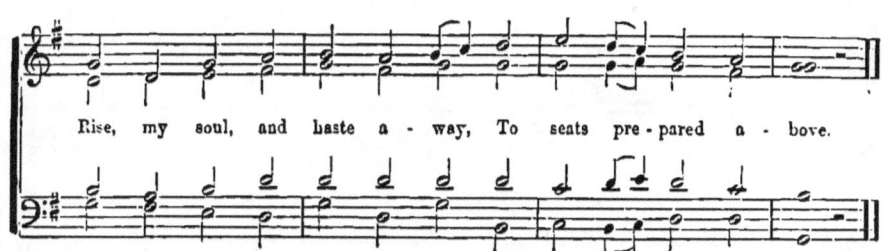

Rise, my soul, and haste a-way, To seats pre-pared a-bove.

2 Cease, my soul, O cease to mourn,
   Press onward to the prize;
Soon the Saviour will return,
   To take thee to the skies:
There is everlasting peace,
   Rest, enduring rest in heaven;
There will sorrow ever cease,
   And crowns of joy be given.

GLORIA PATRI.
To the FATHER, to the SON,
   And SPIRIT ever bless'd,
Everlasting Three in One,
   All worship be address'd:
Praise from all above, below,
   As throughout the ages past,
Now is given, and shall be so
   While endless ages last.

JOY. 7s and 6s. (Peculiar.) 253

252.

From BEETHOVEN's 9th Symphony.
Arranged by EDWARD HODGES, Mus. Doc.

1. Rise, my soul, and stretch thy wings, Thy better portion trace;
2. Cease, my soul, O cease to mourn, Press onward to the prize;

(*Gloria Patri.*) To the FATHER, to the SON, And SPIRIT ever bless'd,

Rise, from transitory things, Towards heaven, thy destined place:
Soon thy Saviour will return, To take thee to the skies:

Everlasting Three in One, All worship be address'd:

Sun, and moon, and stars decay, Time shall soon this earth remove;
There is everlasting peace, Rest, enduring rest in heaven;

Praise from all above, below, As throughout the ages past,

Rise, my soul, and haste away To seats prepared above.
There will sorrow ever cease, And crowns of joy be given.

Now is given, and shall be so, While endless ages last.

"SHOUT THE GLAD TIDINGS."

255. W. H. Walter, 1859.

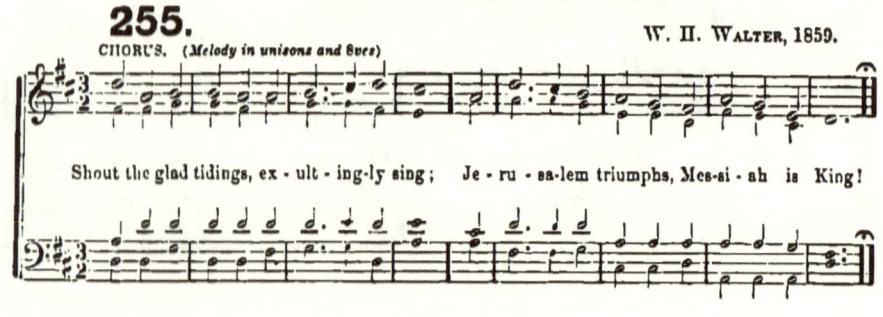

Shout the glad tidings, ex-ult-ing-ly sing; Je-ru-sa-lem triumphs, Mes-si-ah is King!

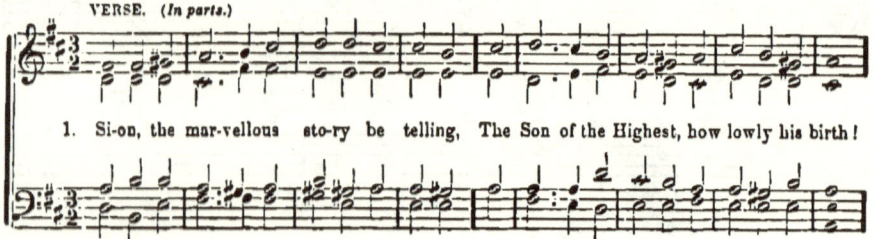

1. Si-on, the mar-vellous sto-ry be telling, The Son of the Highest, how lowly his birth!

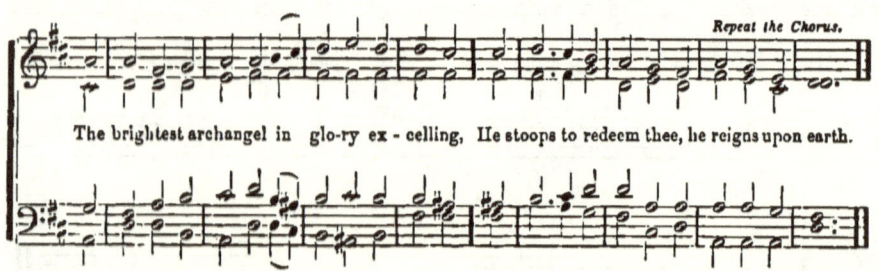

Repeat the Chorus.

The brightest archangel in glo-ry ex-celling, He stoops to redeem thee, he reigns upon earth.

2
Tell how he cometh; from nation to nation,
 The heart-cheering news let the earth echo round;
How free to the faithful he offers salvation,
 How his people with joy everlasting are crown'd.
Cho.—Shout the glad tidings, exultingly sing;
 Jerusalem triumphs, Messiah is King!

3
Mortals, your homage be gratefully bringing,
 And sweet let the gladsome hosanna arise,
Ye angels, the full hallelujah be singing,
 One chorus resound thro' the earth and the skies.
Cho.—Shout the glad tidings, exultingly sing;
 Jerusalem triumphs, Messiah is King!

"VITAL SPARK OF HEAVENLY FLAME."

257.

W. H. Walter. 1860.

1. Vi-tal spark of heavenly flame, Quit, O quit this mor-tal frame; Trembling, hoping, ling'ring, fly-ing, O the pain, the bliss of dy-ing! Cease, fond na-ture, cease thy strife, And let me lan-guish in-to life. 2. Hark, they whis-per, an-gels say, Sis-ter spir-it, come a-way! What is this ab-sorbs me quite;

"VITAL SPARK," Etc. (Concluded.)

"WHEN GATHERING CLOUDS AROUND I VIEW."

(Hypo-Phrygian Mode.)

258.   Rev. J. H. Hopkins, Jr.

1. When gath-ering clouds a-round I view, And days are dark, and friends are few, On Him I lean, who, not in vain, Ex-pe-rienced ev'-ry hu-man pain; He feels my griefs, He sees my fears, And counts and trea-sures up my tears.

2 If aught should tempt my soul to stray
From heavenly wisdom's narrow way,
To fly the good I would pursue,
Or do the ill I would not do;
Still He, who felt temptation's power,
Shall guard me in that dangerous hour.

3 When vexing thoughts within me rise,
And, sore dismay'd, my spirit dies;
Then He, who once vouchsafed to bear
The sickening anguish of despair,
Shall sweetly soothe, shall gently dry
The throbbing heart, the streaming eye.

4 When sorrowing o'er some stone I bend,
Which covers all that was a friend,
And from his voice, his hand, his smile
Divides me for a little while;
Thou, Saviour, seest the tears I shed,
For thou didst weep o'er Lazarus dead.

5 And, oh, when I have safely past
Through every conflict but the last,
Still, still unchanging, watch beside
My bed of death, for thou hast died:
Then point to realms of endless day,
And wipe the latest tear away.

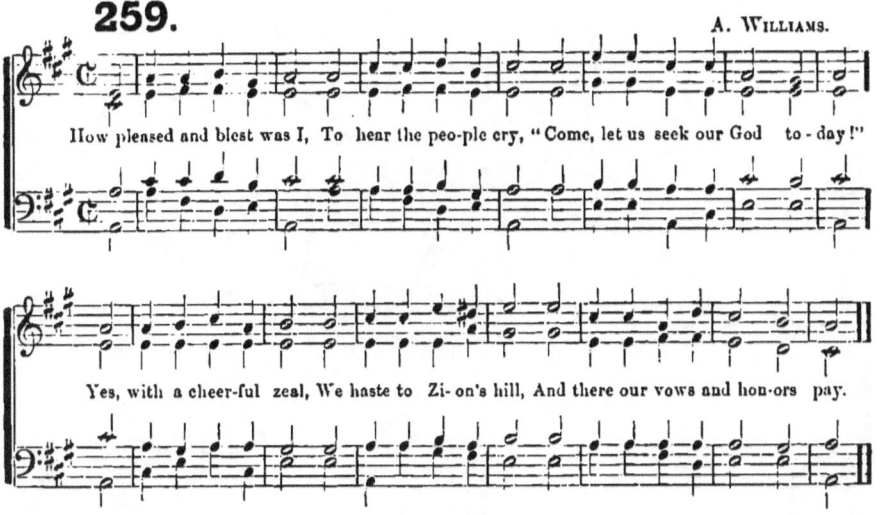

259. DALSTON. S. P. M. (6, 6, 8; 6, 6, 8.) 215
A. Williams.

How pleased and blest was I, To hear the people cry, "Come, let us seek our God to-day!"

Yes, with a cheer-ful zeal, We haste to Zi-on's hill, And there our vows and hon-ors pay.

260. PIERPONT. S. P. M. (6, 6, 8; 6, 6, 8.)
From the "Ancient Lyre."

The Lord Jehovah reigns, And royal state maintains, His head with aw - ful glo-ries crown'd;

Arrayed in robes of light, Begirt with sov'reign might, And rays of ma - jes-ty a - round.

216

261. ST. JEROME'S. S. P. M. (6, 6, 8; 6, 6, 8.)
From the "Ancient Lyre."

Up-held by thy commands, The world secure-ly stands, And skies and stars obey thy word;

Thy throne was fix'd on high, Before the star-ry sky, E-ter-nal is..... thy king-dom, Lord.

E-ter-nal is thy king-dom, Lord.

262. ST. THERESA. S. L. M. (6, 6; 8, 6; 8, 8.)
W. H. Walter, 1860.

Friend af-ter friend de-parts; Who hath not lost a friend!

There is no u-nion here of hearts, That finds not here an end;

ST. THERESA. (Concluded.) 217

Were this frail world our on - ly rest, Liv - ing or dy - ing, none were blest.

263. WILSON. C. L. M. (8, 6, 8, 6; 8, 8.)
JOACHIM VON BURK. 1580.

Heav'n is the land where trou-bles cease, Where toils and tears are o'er,

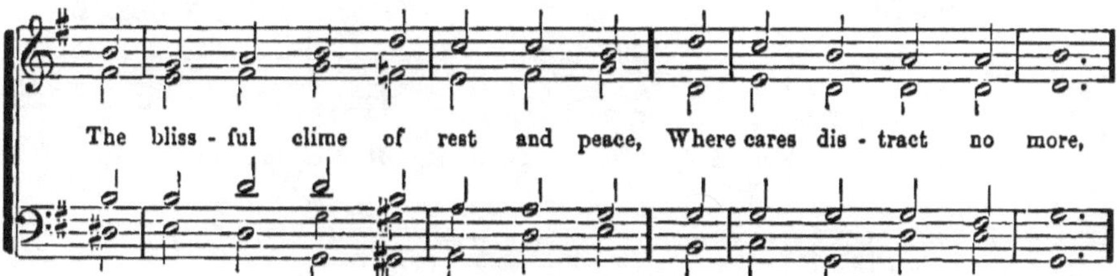

The bliss - ful clime of rest and peace, Where cares dis - tract no more,

And not the sha - dow of dis - tress Dims its un - sul - lied bless - ed - ness.

264. AMERICA. 6s & 4s.

A NATIONAL ANTHEM.

Thou, whose Al-migh-ty word, Cha-os and darkness heard, And took their flight! Hear us, we humbly pray; And where the gospel day Sheds not its glo-rious ray, Let there be light!

265. ITALIAN HYMN. 6s & 4s.

F. GIARDINI.

Come, thou Almigh-ty King, Help us Thy name to sing, Help us to praise! Fa-ther all glo-ri-ous, O'er all vic-to-ri-ous, Come, and reign o-ver us, An-cient of days.

"BRIGHTEST AND BEST." Etc.

266. Melody from SAM'L WEBBE.

"THERE IS AN HOUR OF HALLOWED PEACE."

267. THEO. H. SMITH.

"THOU ART GONE TO THE GRAVE."

268.

From a GERMAN CHORAL.

Thou art gone to the grave! but we will not de-plore thee, Tho' sor-row and dark-ness en-com-pass the tomb! The Sa-viour has pass'd through its por-tals be-fore thee, And the lamp of His love is thy guide thro' the gloom.

2 Thou art gone to the grave! we no
    longer behold thee,
Nor tread the rough paths of the
    world by thy side;
But the wide arms of mercy are
    spread to enfold thee,
And sinners may die, for the
    Sinless hath died.

3 Thou art gone to the grave! and its
    mansion forsaking,
What though thy weak spirit in
    fear lingered long;
The sunshine of Paradise beamed
    on thy waking,
And the sound which thou heards't
    was the Seraphim's song.

4 Thou art gone to the grave! but we will not deplore thee,
    For God was thy Ransom, thy Guardian, and Guide:
He gave thee, He took thee, and He will restore thee;
    And death hath no sting, for the Saviour hath died.

INDEX TO SINGLE CHANTS.

Composer.	Key.	No.	Composer.	Key.	No.	Composer.	Key.	No.
Arnold	B♭	70	Hine	G	16	Tallis	F	1
Ayrton	E♭	74	Humphrey	C	83	Travers	E	67
Blow	E minor	68				"	E	77
Crotch	B♭	73	Nares	A	38	Tucker	A	72
"	D	80	Novello	B♭	40	Turner	A	78
Dupuis	E♭	81	"	B♭	60	Uncertain	B♭	3
Felton	E♭	43	"	A	66	"	B♭	37
"	F	79	Purcell	G	64	"	E	63
Farrant	G minor	9	Russell	C	62	Walter	G minor	61
"	F	15	"	C	76	"	E♭	71
Fussell	G	41	"	F	82	"	E minor	75
Hayes	D	65						

INDEX TO DOUBLE CHANTS.

Composer.	Key.	No.	Composer.	Key.	No.	Composer.	Key.	No.
Aldrich	F	12	Handel	G	25	Uncertain	C	19
Attwood	D	23	Jackson	B♭	11	"	F	24
Barrow	G	49	Jones	C	44	"	B♭	33
Battishill	D	14	Langdon	F	2	"	E♭	35
Bennett	F	10	Morley	D minor	42	"	E	36
Boyce	D	5	Mornington	E	7	"	G	53
Crotch	C	52	"	E♭	21	Walter	B♭	17
Dupuis	E♭	27	Norris	A	32	"	G	22
"	E	46	Pratt	E	13	"	A♭	29
"	A	48	Randall	E	20	"	E	30
Flintoft	F minor	59	Robinson	E♭	6	"	E♭	31
Hayes	G	4	Russell	E♭	51	"	B♭	39
Hodges	G	9	Smith	C	56	"	B♭	45
"	F	18	Soaper	D	47	"	A	50
"	D	26	Spencer	D	34	"	E♭	54
"	G	58	Teesdale	E	28	"	G	57
Higgins	F	55						

INDEX TO CANTICLES.

VENITE, EXULTEMUS.

Tallis	F	1
Langdon	F	2
Gregorian	B♭	3
Hayes	G	4
Boyce	D	5
Robinson	E♭	6
Mornington	E	7

GLORIA IN EXCELSIS.

Triple Chant	G	8

TE DEUM LAUDAMUS.

Hodges	G	9

BENEDICITE.

Bennett	F	10

JUBILATE DEO.

Jackson	B♭	11
Aldrich	F	12
Pratt	E	13
Battishill	D	14

BENEDICTUS.

Farrant	F	15
Hine	G	16
Walter	B♭	17
Hodges	F	18
Unknown	C	19

CANTATE DOMINO.

Randall	E	20
Mornington	E♭	21
Walter	G	22
Attwood	D	23

BONUM EST CONFITERI.

Uncertain	F	24
Handel	G	25
Hodges	D	26
Dupuis	E♭	27

DEUS MISEREATUR.

Teesdale	E	28
Walter	A♭	29

Walter	E	30
"	E♭	31

BENEDIC, ANIMA MEA.

Norris	A	32
Uncertain	B	33
Spencer	D	34
Uncertain	E♭	35

EASTER DAY.

Unknown	E	36
Gregorian	B♭	37
Nares	A	38

THANKSGIVING DAY.

Walter	B♭	39
Novello	B♭	40
Fussell	G	41

BURIAL OF THE DEAD.

Morley	D minor	42
Felton	E♭	43

METRICAL INDEX TO THE TUNES.

C. M.

Tune	No.	Page	Tune	No.	Page	Tune	No.	Page
Abbey,	1	61	Redemption,	46	84	97th Psalm Tune,	92	108
Abridge,	2	62	Salisbury, (old,)	47	"	Old 100th,	93	"
Alexandria,	3	"	Stade,	48	85	Playford,	94	109
Approbation,	4	63	St. Alban's,	49	"	Prague,	95	"
Arden,	5	"	St. Ann's,	50	86	Rockingham,	96	110
Bangor,	6	64	St. Elisabeth,	51	"	Rogers,	97	"
Barby,	7	"	St. James',	52	87	Samson,	98	111
Bedford, $\frac{3}{2}$	8	65	St. Luke's,	53	"	Seasons,	99	"
" $\mathbb{C}$	9	"	St. Magnus, (*Notting-ham*.)	54	88	Sebastian,	100	112
Belgrave,	10	66	St. Mary's,	55	"	Spring,	101	"
Benediction,	11	"	St. Stephen's,	56	89	Stonefield,	102	113
Braintree,	12	"	Swanwick,	57	"	Surrey,	103	"
Bristol,	13	"	Tallis,	58	90	St. Augustine,	104	114
Brunswick,	14	"	Thaxted,	59	"	St. Bartholomew's,	105	"
Burford,	15	"	Tiverton,	60	91	St. Basil,	106	115
Burlington,	16	69	Trinity Chapel,	61	"	St. Chrysostom,	107	"
Carlisle,	17	"	Tottenham,	62	92	St. George's,	108	116
Chelsea,	18	70	Tye,	63	"	St. Pancras,	109	"
Chesterfield,	19	"	Vulpius	64	93	St. Paul's,	110	117
Chestnut Ridge,	20	"	Windsor,	65	"	St. Peters,	111	"
Chichester,	21	"	York,	66	94	Tallis' Canon,	112	118
Christmas,	22	72	Zurich,	67	"	" Evening Hymn,	113	"
Christ's Hospital,	23	"				Towner,	114	119
Colchester,	24	73	**C. M. Double.**			Trinity,	115	"
Coventry,	25	"	Dungeness,	68	95	Truro,	116	120
Dantzic	26	74	Tolland,	69	96	Vienna, (*Germany*.)	117	"
Dumferline,	27	"	**L. M.**			Wells,	118	121
Dundee,	28	75	All Saints,	70	97	Whiteland,	119	"
Eckardtsheim,	29	"	Almin,	71	"	Winchester, $\frac{3}{2}$	120	122
Farrant,	30	76	Angel's Hymn,	72	98	" $\mathbb{C}$	121	"
Funeral Hymn,	31	"	Ascension,	73	"	Windham,	122	123
Gregorian,	32	77	Atlantic,	74	99	Wittenberg,	123	"
Havana,	33	"	Bartholdy,	75	"	**L. M. Double.**		
Jubal,	34	"	Benevolence,	76	100	Creation,	124	124
Limburg,	35	78	Berlin,	77	"	**S. M.**		
London,	36	"	Blendon,	78	101	Asaph,	125	125
Lutzen,	37	"	Bowen,	79	"	Aylesbury,	126	"
Manchester,	38	80	Coburg,	80	102	Boyce,	127	126
Martyrdom,	39	"	Duke Street,	81	"	Cambridge,	128	"
Martyrs,	40	81	Elno,	82	103	Carlisle,	129	127
Mear,	41	"	Grace Church,	83	"	Christ's Church,	130	"
Messiah,	42	"	Hamburg,	84	104	Croydon, (*Tytherton*,)	152	138
Nayland,	43	"	High Street,	85	"	Denant,	131	128
Norton,	44	"	Kemper,	86	105	Doncaster,	132	"
Nottingham, (*St. Magnus*),	54	83	Luton,	87	"	Fairfield,	133	129
			Mendon,	88	106	Gibbons,	134	"
			Morning Hymn,	89	"	Gorton,	135	130
Old English Tune,	45	83	Mozart,	90	107	Handel,	136	"
			Nazareth,	91	"			

	No.	Page.		No.	Page.		No.	Page.
Hindsley,	137	131	**II. 5, or 10s.**			Trust,	227	189
Kidderminster,	138	"		No.	Page.	Waltham,	228	190
Kirkdale,	139	132	Calcott,	185	163	Worthing,	229	"
Mornington,	140	"	Refuge,	186	"	**III. 3, or 8s and 7s, Double.**		
Olmutz,	141	133	Russian Hymn,	187	164	Adoration,	230	191
Paddington,	142	"	St. Clement's,	188	"	"Love Divine,"	231	192
Peace,	143	134	**II. 6, or 7s & 6s.**			Mantua,	232	193
Pentonville,	144	"	Epiphany,	189	165	**III. 4.**		
Schumann,	145	135	Melchior,	190	166	Edom,	233	194
Shirland,	146	"	Romaine,	191	167	Vision,	234	195
St. Benedict,	147	136	**II. 7, or 8 & 7s IRREGULAR.**			**III. 5, or 8s, 7s & 4s.**		
St. Bride's,	148	"	Judgment Hymn,	192	168	Advent Hymn,	235	196
St. Laurence,	149	137	**II. 8.**			Canterbury,	219	185
St. Michael's,	150	"	St. Paul's Chapel,	193	169	Edom,	233	194
St. Thomas',	151	138	**III. 1, or 7s.**			Erpingham,	236	196
Tytberton, (Croydon,)	152	"	Angelus,	194	170	Haydn's Hymn,	237	197
S. M. Double.			Bloomfield,	195	"	Joanna,	238	198
Altenburg,	153	139	Breslau,	196	171	Novello,	239	"
Holstein,	154	140	During,	197	"	Oriel,	240	199
Prayer,	155	141	Edyfield,	198	172	Salvation,	225	188
II. 1 or C. P. M.			Easter Hymn,	256	211	Sicilian Hymn,	226	189
Bethany,	156	142	Even-Song,	199	172	**IV. 1, or 5s & 6s.**		
Guilbert,	157	143	Innocents,	200	173	Hanover,	241	200
Habakkuk,	158	144	Gloria Patri,	201	"	Lyons,	242	"
Harwood,	159	145	Magdalen,	202	174	**IV. 2, or 8s.**		
Treves,	160	146	Nuremberg,	203	"	Devotion,	243	201
II. 2 or L. P. M.			Pleyel's Hymn,	204	175	Goshen,	244	"
Berne,	161	147	Sharon,	205	"	**IV. 3.**		
Madison,	162	148	St, Aiden's,	206	176	St. Polycarp,	245	202
Melchisedec,	163	149	St. Ambrose,	207	"	**IV. 4, or 11s.**		
Newcourt,	164	150	Theodora,	208	177	"Adeste Fideles,"	247	203
Ravenscroft,	165	151	Weber,	209	"	Faith,	248	204
II. 3, or L. M. 6 lines.			**III. 1, or 7s, Double.**			Welcome,	246	202
Brownell,	166	152	Cecil,	210	178	**IV. 5, or 12s.**		
Carey's Tune,	167	"	Hotham,	211	179	Erfurt,	249	204
Dresden,	168	153	Rapture,	212	180	**7s and 6s. (Peculiar).**		
Eaton,	169	154	St. Asaph,	213	181	Amsterdam,	250	205
Griswold,	170	"	**III. 2, or 7s, SIX LINES.**			Hope,	251	206
Mainz,	171	155	Alleluia,	214	182	Joy,	252	207
Salisbury,	172	156	Cecil,	210	178	**6s, 8s and 4s.**		
St. Stephen,	173	"	Gethsemane,	215	182	Leoni,	253	208
II. 4, or H. M.			Gratitude,	216	183	Praise,	254	209
Bethesda,	174	157	"Rock of Ages,"	217	184	**6s and 4s.**		
Daniell,	175	158	**III. 3, or 8s & 7s.**			America,	264	218
Darwell,	176	"	Anfield,	218	185	Italian Hymn,	265	"
Irenaeus,	177	"	Canterbury,	219	"	**S. P. M.**		
Leipsic,	178	159	Cheetham,	220	186	Dalston,	259	215
Minster,	179	160	Frankfort,	221	"	Pierpont,	260	"
Psalm 148,	180	"	Havergal,	222	187	St. Jerome,	261	216
St. John's,	181	161	Manheim,	223	"	**S. L. M.**		
St. Philips,	182	"	Merton,	224	188	St. Theresa,	262	216
Triumph,	183	162	Salvation,	225	"	**C. L. M.**		
Warsaw,	184	"	Sharon,	205	175	Wilson,	263	217
			Sicilian Hymn,	226	189			

ALPHABETICAL INDEX TO THE TUNES.

A.
Tune	Page
Abbey,	61
Abridge,	62
Adeste Fideles,	203
Adoration,	191
Advent Hymn,	196
Alexandria,	62
Alleluia,	182
All Saints,	97
Almin,	97
Altenburg,	189
America,	218
Amsterdam,	205
Anfield,	188
Angel's Hymn,	98
Angelus,	170
Approbation,	63
Arden,	63
Asaph,	125
Ascension,	98
Atlantic,	99
Aylesbury,	125

B.
Bangor,	64
Barby,	64
Bartholdy,	99
Bedford,	65
Belgrave,	66
Benediction,	66
Benevolence,	100
Berlin,	100
Berne,	147
Bethany,	142
Bethesda,	157
Blendon,	101
Bloomfield,	170
Bowen,	101
Boyce,	126
Braintree,	67
Breslau,	171
Brightest and Best,	219
Brist ol,	67
Brownell,	152
Brunswick,	68
Burford,	68
Burlington,	69

C.
Calcott,	168
Cambridge,	126
Canterbury,	188
Carey's Tune,	152
Carlisle, (C. M.,)	49
Carlisle, (S. M.,)	127
Cecil,	175
Cheetham,	186
Chelsea,	70
Chesterfield,	70
Chestnut Ridge,	71
Chichester,	71
Christmas,	72
Christ's Church,	127
Christ's Hospital,	72
Coburg,	102
Colchester,	73
Coventry,	73
Creation,	124
Croydon,	138

D.
Tune	Page
Dalston,	215
Dantell,	158
Dantzic,	74
Darwell,	159
Denbah,	123
Devotion,	201
Doncaster,	128
Dresden,	153

Tune	Page
Duke Street,	102
Dumferline,	74
Dundee,	75
Dungeness,	95
Düring,	171

E.
Tune	Page
Easter Hymn,	211
Eaton,	154
Eckardtsheim,	75
Edom,	194
Elyfield,	172
Elno,	103
Epiphany,	165
Erfort,	204
Erpingham,	106
Even-Song,	172

F.
Tune	Page
Fairfield,	129
Faith,	204
Farrant,	76
Frankfort,	186
Funeral Hymn,	76

G.
Germany,	120
Gethsemane,	182
Gibbons,	129
Gloria Patri,	173
Gloria Tibi,	60
Gorton,	130
Goshen,	201
Grace Church,	103
Gratitude,	188
Gregorian,	77
Griswold,	154
Guilbert,	143

H.
Tune	Page
Habakkuk,	144
Hamburg,	104
Handel,	130
Hanover,	200
Harwood,	145
Havana,	77
Haveryal,	187
Haydn's Hymn,	197
High Street,	104
Hindsley,	131
Holstein,	140
Hope,	206
Hotham,	179

I.
Innocents,	178
Irenæus,	159
Italian Hymn,	218

J.
Joanna,	198
Joy,	207
Jubal,	78
Judgment Hymn,	165

K.
Kemper,	105
Kidderminster,	131
Kirkdale,	132
Kyrie Eleison,	60

L.
Leipsic,	150
Leoni,	208
Limburg,	78
London,	79
Love Divine,	192
Luton,	105
Lutzen,	79

Tune	Page
Lyons,	200

M.
Tune	Page
Madison,	148
Magdalen,	174
Mainz,	155
Manchester,	80
Manheim,	157
Mantua,	193
Martyrdom,	80
Martyrs,	81
Mear,	81
Melchisedec,	149
Melchior,	166
Mendon,	106
Merton,	188
Messiah,	82
Minster,	160
Morning Hymn,	106
Mornington,	182
Mozart,	107

N.
Tune	Page
Nayland,	82
Nazareth,	107
Newcourt,	150
Ninety-Seventh Psalm Tune,	108
Norton,	83
Nottingham,	88
Novello,	198
Nuremberg,	174

O.
Old English Tune,	83
Old Hundredth,	108
Olmutz,	133
Oriel,	199

P.
Paddington,	133
Peace,	184
Pentonville,	134
Pierpont,	215
Playford,	109
Pleyel's Hymn,	175
Praise,	209
Prague,	109
Prayer,	141
Psalm 148,	160

R.
Rapture,	150
Ravenscroft,	151
Redemption,	84
Refuge,	163
Rockingham,	110
Rock of Ages,	179
Rogers,	110
Romaine,	167
Russian Hymn,	164

S.
Salisbury, (Old,)	84
Salisbury, (New,)	156
Salvation,	188
Samson,	111
Sanctus,	60
Schumann,	135
Seasons,	111
Sebastian,	112
Sharon,	175
Shirland,	135
Sicilian Hymn,	180
Spring,	112
Shade,	85
St. Alden's,	176
St. Alban's,	65
St. Ambrose,	176

Tune	Page
St. Ann's,	66
St. Asaph,	181
St. Augustine,	114
St. Bartholomew's,	114
St. Basil,	115
St. Benedict,	186
St. Bride's,	186
St. Chrysostom,	115
St. Clement's,	164
St. Elizabeth,	148
St. George's,	116
St. James',	87
St. Jerome's,	216
St. John's,	161
St. Laurence,	137
St. Luke's,	67
St. Magnus,	88
St. Mary's,	89
St. Michael's,	137
St. Pancras,	116
St. Paul's,	117
St. Paul's Chapel,	169
St. Peter's,	117
St. Philip's,	161
St. Polycarp,	202
St. Stephen's,	89
St. Stephen,	156
St. Theresa,	216
St. Thomas,	136
Stonefield,	113
Surrey,	113
Swanwick,	69

T.
Tallis,	90
Tallis' Canon,	118
Tallis' Ev. Hymn,	118
Thaxted,	90
Theodora,	177
There is an Hour,	219
Thou art gone,	220
Tiverton,	91
Tolland,	96
Tottenham,	92
Towner,	119
Treves,	146
Trinity,	119
Trinity Chapel,	91
Triumph,	162
Truro,	120
Trust,	189
Tye,	92
Tytherton,	138

V.
Tune	Page
Vienna,	120
Vision,	195
Vulpius,	93

W.
Waltham,	190
Warsaw,	162
Weber,	177
Welcome,	202
Wells,	121
Whiteland,	121
Wilson,	217
Winchester,	122
Windham,	123
Windsor,	93
Wittenbury,	123
Worthing,	190

Y.
Tune	Page
York,	94

Z.
Zurich,	94

www.ingramcontent.com/pod-product-compliance
Lightning Source LLC
Chambersburg PA
CBHW021840230426
43669CB00008B/1030